Michael Legat began writing w
entered the world of publishing
of his working life. During thi
his own published, a highly acclaimed
and also translated various works. In 1978, having gained a distinguished reputation in the publishing industry, he decided to resign his position as editorial director and devote himself to writing full time. His first novel, *Mario's Vineyard* was published with great success in 1980, and a series of further novels followed.

The president of two writers' circles, he is also a popular and entertaining speaker at writers' conferences, and he has considerable experience as a tutor of creative writing. He has served on the management committee of the Society of Authors, and as a Director both of the Authors' Licensing and Collecting Society and of the Copyright Licensing Agency. He lives with his wife in Horsted Keynes, West Sussex.

BY MICHAEL LEGAT
ALL PUBLISHED BY HOUSE OF STRATUS

Mario's Vineyard
The Silk Maker
The Cast Iron Man
The Shapiro Diamond
The Silver Fountain

Legat's Writing Guides:
- Plotting The Novel
- Writng Historical Novels
- Writing Non-Fiction
- Writing Your Life Story

Michael Legat

WRITING HISTORICAL NOVELS

HOUSE OF STRATUS

This edition published in 2011 by House of Stratus, an imprint of Stratus Books Ltd., Lisandra House, Fore Street, Looe, Cornwall, PL13 1AD, U.K.

www.houseofstratus.com

Typeset, printed and bound by House of Stratus.

A catalogue record for this book is available from the British Library and the Library of Congress.

ISBN 0-7551-2662-9

1

A MATTER OF CHOICE

The popularity of historical novels is unquestioned. Occasionally you will hear that publishers have decided that their day is over, but somehow they continue to appear.

What is the secret of their appeal? All fiction is to some extent escapist – it takes us away from our own lives and into those of other people. And what could be more escapist than to travel in your reading into the past, when life was less hectic than today, when people were not constantly harassed by all the pressures of modern life? For most of us the past is glamorous.

However, if we were transported back by some time-machine, we should probably discover that life in bygone days was thoroughly unpleasant for the majority of people, at least by our own modern standards, and that its problems, though different from our own, were just as acute. Be that as it may, for readers of historical novels the past is colourful and picturesque, and even if the author tries to present the squalor, the misery, the brutality in realistic terms, the glamour somehow remains, simply because the reader is taken into a different world.

The 'historical novel' as we know it today may be said to have been invented by Sir Walter Scott, who was the first major author to set some of his novels in the distant past. Until he began doing so, unless you count a few works such as Malory's *Morte D'Arthur* as historical novels, novelists had written contemporary stories only. The genre caught on and nowadays historical novels abound, ranging in period from the beginning of time up to the end of the nineteenth century. Some people also refer to stories set in the first twenty or thirty years of the twentieth century as 'historicals', but even though we are talking of a time which is now well over half a century ago, others prefer to categorise such books as 'period' rather than 'historical', and, indeed, would prefer to demand that a setting should, like an antique, be at least a hundred years old before the story could be called 'historical'.

So why do *you* want to write a historical novel? Perhaps you have the same tastes as Miss Trant in J. B. Priestley's *The Good Companions* (itself now at least a period piece, if it cannot justifiably be called historical):

> She had a passion for historical romances, not silly sentimental stories passing themselves off under cover of a few cloaks and daggers and 'halidoms' or 'Odds-fish', but real full-blooded historical tales. These she preferred to any other kind of fiction, and for the last twenty years they had been first her delight and then her solace. She loved to carry a secret message from Louis the Eleventh of France to Charles, Duke of Burgundy; to peep out of a haystack at Ireton's troopers; to hide in the heather after Prince Charlie had taken ship to France; to go thundering over the Rhine with Napoleon and his marshals. To exchange passwords, to rally the horse on the left, to clatter down the Great North Road, to hammer upon inn doors on nights of wind and sleet,

these were the pleasures of her imagination.

If you want to write a historical novel because you enjoy reading them, that is the best of justifications. But you do not necessarily have to like or want to write the kind of book that Priestley describes. Historical novels come in great variety, and they do not all involve real-life characters, or the kind of wild adventures that include clattering down the Great North Road and hammering upon inn doors on nights of wind and sleet.

The various types of historical novel are not always completely clear-cut, but they could perhaps be classified as follows.

(i) *Central character is a well-known historical personage*

This is typically a story about, say, Henry VIII (and any one or all of his wives), or Warwick the Kingmaker, or Elizabeth Fry. It does not, of course, have to be confined to English men and women, and could be about Christopher Columbus, Ivan the Terrible, Confucius, Thomas Jefferson, or anyone else you can think of. It is, however, the essence of this kind of story that, although many fictional episodes may be added, and the emotions of the characters may be imaginatively explored, it is firmly based on historical fact. If you were to choose Henry VIII as your principal character, the novel might concentrate on his private life to the exclusion of affairs of State, but you would not change him into a short, weedy and indecisive individual, nor allow him to be dallying with one of the ladies of the Court when in fact he would have been at the Field of the Cloth of Gold. The novel can extend over quite a long period, when it almost turns into a biography made fictional by the introduction of imaginative dialogue, and the dramatizing of the more exciting aspects of the subject's life and the elimination of the duller bits. Equally, it can be concerned only with a comparatively brief event which provides the historical central character with a moment of crisis. Among its cast of characters there may be some whom the author has invented, but there will certainly be many of those who actually lived and worked with the main protagonist.

A variation on this is the novel which creates a wholly fictional episode in the life of a historical personage. An author might, for instance, decide that Henry VIII must have had many affairs with young ladies apart from those he married, and could perhaps invent the Lady Mary Whatshername, who has a torrid few weeks with the king before he throws her over in favour of Katherine Howard. But again, the author will not depart too far from historical fact, and must try to keep all the background details as authentic as possible.

(ii) *Central characters are all imaginary*

In many ways, this kind of story gives much more freedom than the previous one. All that is truly historical here is the period, the background against which the story is set. It can be a simple love story, or anything else that the author wants it to be. The basic plot could possibly be transposed to any period at all, but it is set at a time which the author has researched and likes, and which gives the opportunity for colourful and picturesque descriptions.

Moreover, the author has, or should have, chosen that particular period because it does affect the story in some way. In some cases, the major historical events of the age may not greatly impinge on the characters, thus giving the author the ability to concentrate solely on their relationships (even as late as the eighteenth century there must have been many people who lived out their entire lives in ignorance of the events which we now read about in history books), but the social conditions of the period will certainly be reflected in the story. Historical real-life characters may appear in it – the hero and heroine might, for example, watch Mary Queen of Scots pass through their village on her way to Fotheringhay – but they will probably only make brief appearances, and will play no major part in the action of the novel.

(iii) *Where the background is as important as the characters*

I am thinking here, not surprisingly perhaps, of my own novels, all of which have been set in the nineteenth century, and all of which have some kind of industry, described with as much accuracy as I could contrive, against which the imaginary characters are set, as a major element in the story. So *Mario's Vineyard* is about growing vines and making wine. *The Silver Fountain* is about the restaurant business, *The Shapiro Diamond* about the early days of diamond-digging in Kimberley, and *The Silk Maker* and *The Cast Iron Man* about the manufacture of silk and of cast iron respectively. True-life historical events can, and do, have their effect on the characters, but play only a minor part. The background which forms an essential ingredient in such stories does not, of course, have to be industrial – it could equally be a war, or a voyage of exploration, or anything else in which the characters are deeply engaged.

(iv) *The Family Saga*

In these books we are almost always concerned with a fictional family, and although the story may be set in past times, the interest is basically in the various incidents within the family which provide the dramatic content of the book, rather than with major historical events. For instance, a war may claim the life of a son, but there is usually no attempt to explain the causes of the war or to chart its course; it exists in the book solely, as it were, for the purpose of removing one of the characters. The main characteristic of the family saga is that it covers more than one generation of the family, and follows in some detail the lives of several of the family's members. The most successful family sagas nowadays are those which are centred on an indomitable woman, who often develops into a matriarchal figure.

(v) *The Romantic Historical Novel*

This is usually a standard romance plot, in which the heroine ends up in the arms of the hero (usually with marriage and a happily-ever-after life in prospect), after many misunderstandings and intrigues and escapes from unsuitable suitors. Frequently, she is betrothed by her parents to an elderly aristocrat of unpleasant appearance and habits, and it takes a great deal of ingenuity on the part of all concerned, including the author, before she can free herself from this entanglement. The most notable form of this kind of historical novel is the Regency Romance, of which the mistress was Georgette Heyer. The stories may have been a little lightweight, and if this is the kind of book you want to write, you may think that the period background is of comparatively minor importance. If so, you are wrong. Follow Georgette Heyer's example – the historical details in her books were always meticulously researched.

(vi) *The Gothic Novel*

The prototype of this form is *Jane Eyre*, which of course was a contemporary story when it was written. The genre had a brief vogue a few years ago, when the majority of those published were given twentieth-century settings. Some, however, had a historical background. All of them had the same basic elements – a young and frightened woman, a large and forbidding house, and an apparently cold and even vicious young man who, naturally, turned out in the end to be kind, warm-hearted and desperately in love with the heroine.

(vii) *The Historical Adventure Novel*

This is the kind that Miss Trant liked, full of swash and with plenty of buckle. It does indeed describe flights, and clashing swords, and deeds of derring-do, not to mention clattering down the Great North Road, and most of the characters will have cloaks under which to conceal their daggers. The principal character will almost certainly be fictitious, male, handsome and devil-may-care – quite capable of fighting off a horde of his enemies single-handed – and virtually every woman he meets will fall madly in love with him.

The historical adventure novel is often rather short on historical accuracy and general believability. Moving at breakneck speed, excitement following excitement without pause, it keeps its breathless readers turning the pages, and they may not care a great deal if the hero's adventures are incredible, if the dialogue is full of modern slang, and if the historical background has been shamelessly distorted. However, it is possible, and vastly preferable, to write this kind of novel without such sloppiness.

(viii) *The Bodice-Ripper*

This is in some ways a kind of female equivalent of the adventure novel. In the latter, the main character makes things happen. In the bodice-ripper, the central figure is a young and attractive woman, and it is not so much the case that she makes things happen as that things happen to her. She does, of course, make them happen in one sense, simply by being an attractive female, with the kind of face and figure that send men wild with lust, and by placing herself regularly in a situation in which that lust can be gratified. She is repeatedly ravished, and not unnaturally the encounters often begin with her bodice being ripped.

The bodice-ripper is a comparatively new form. It could be said that the first of the genre in modern times was Kathleen Winsor's *Forever Amber,* but Amber was never seen beyond the door to the bedroom into which she disappeared with her latest lover. The bodice-ripper, on the other hand, conceals little, and sometimes approaches outright pornography.

Like the historical adventure novel, the bodice-ripper is often extraordinarily badly written, with pasteboard characters, anachronistic dialogue, and a plot in which each succeeding incident is harder to swallow than its predecessor. Even the sex scenes tend to be banal. However, the wretched things do sell.

Making Your Choice

The choice is huge. As well as the forms listed above, there are other variations too, such as a crime novel with a historical setting, like the splendid stories by Ellis Peters about the Benedictine monk, Brother Cadfael, or Peter Lovesey's equally excellent Victorian thrillers featuring Sergeant Cribb.

One thing that all successful historical novels have in common is that their stories could not be set in any other age than that which the author has chosen – in other words, the period affects the characters and their actions and the events in which they are caught up. Take a simple love story, set it in different periods, and the attitudes, the social and historical backgrounds of the time will transform it in each case – or should do.

As has already been said, it is not always easy to categorise a given historical novel – the family saga may have a background of industry which becomes, as it were, a character in the story, while if you centre your story on a real-life character such as the pirate Captain Kidd, it may well be packed with action and qualify as an adventure story. When asked to describe my own novels I say they are historical, since they are all set in the nineteenth century; they are romances, since as in Miss Prism's definition of fiction, the good end happily and the bad unhappily; they are family sagas, since they cover more than one generation of the families in them; and they are industrial novels, because the business in which the characters are concerned always plays a big part in the stories. So you may well wish to combine various types of story.

You may ask which genre is most likely to be accepted for publication. Well, you can study trends, by doing your market research in libraries and bookshops, and then try to write something that you think will be popular. That's all right, if your heart is in it, but you are less likely to succeed if you don't really believe in what you are doing and are simply trying to satisfy an unknown editor. You should always write first and foremost to please yourself – write the kind of book that you would like to read, set in a period that fascinates you, and telling a story that can only be set at that particular time, and you'll give yourself a head start.

Would-be novelists in all genres worry about originality. There are said to be only half a dozen or so basic plots, and originality is often to be found only in characterisations and settings. Here the historical novelist has a great advantage, having several millennia to choose from – or at least close on a score of centuries which have been well documented, so that adequate research is possible. Try to be original in your choice of period and background and characters. Give your imagination free rein, and then back it up by careful research. It is sometimes helpful for beginners to try to mould themselves on a popular author whose books they enjoy, but that approach should be used only as an exercise to get you going. Once you set out in earnest to write your historical novel, try to find your own voice, so that however ordinary your basic plot may be, the novel will have originality simply because *you* have written it.

Length and Style

Whichever form a historical novel may take, it can be of any length (although the Historical Romance is unlikely to be longer than, say, 60,000 words). Family sagas often run to around 200,000 words, because they have a large cast of characters and each member of the family may have his or her own individual and complex story woven into the main narrative. Some authors, like James Michener and James Clavell regularly produce enormously long historical novels, containing half a million words or more.

It is difficult to give guidance on how long your own book should be, since it depends on the complexity of the story you are telling, the number of characters and sub-plots, and, perhaps, the time-span of the novel. All that can be said with certainty is that it should be as long as it needs to be to tell its story effectively – it should neither be underwritten, nor padded. You may find some resistance among publishers to either a very short book or a very long one, and you will probably stand most chance with a book of between 50,000 and 100,000 words. Having said that, if your book is well researched, well written, has that essential page-turning quality, and at least a modicum of originality, you should have a fair chance of finding a publisher for it, even if it runs to a quarter of a million words or more.

The majority of historical novels will be popular in style – typically providing 'a good read' – but they can also be scholarly and Literary with a capital L. They can be romantic in approach – history without the warts, as it were – or they can be realistic, unflinchingly presenting all the more unpleasant aspects of bygone ages – the squalor, the disease, the poverty. They can be highly selective in the events they cover, or can attempt to give a comprehensive account of life at that particular time.

2

PLANNING

Historical novels differ from other kinds of novel principally in the obvious fact that they are set in bygone periods. There is a possible difference in the greater amount of research which may have to be done, and you will certainly need to write your dialogue in a way which avoids any sense of twentieth-century forms of speech, and to make every effort to produce a strong sense of the age in question and to get the period details right. Rhona Martin, whose novel *Gallows Wedding* won the Georgette Heyer Historical Novel Prize, points out that the storyline and the characters must be very strong – readers expect plenty of colour and drama in the stories.

However, in many ways the writing of a historical novel demands exactly the same approach as that of any other novel. A novel is a novel is a novel, as Gertrude Stein might have said, and basically they are all constructed in the same way. The advice contained in this book is therefore in many respects identical with that which I would give to any writer of fiction, whatever genre he or she might be attempting.

The first thing that I would say to a would-be novelist (or indeed to anyone who wants to write a book of any kind) is that you should begin by planning your work.

I am a great believer in the value to an author of a detailed synopsis. While I acknowledge that some writers cannot work in this way, preferring to start writing without being sure how the story will end, I would like to persuade beginners, in particular, to plan their books in advance of the actual writing.

There are several advantages in so doing. The most important, perhaps, is that in this way you can give *shape* to your story, and that is a subject to which I shall return later. Secondly, it always seems to me to help to know where you are going – the ending of your book, when you know it (and I have usually written the last line of my novels before I have written the first one), becomes a goal towards which you drive. Thirdly, a synopsis helps to eradicate 'writer's block', which often occurs not so much because for some reason your mind is reluctant to let you write, but because you are making the story up as you go along and have reached a point where you don't really know what happens next. As a kind of variation on this point, and a bonus, I find that a synopsis helps me to get back to writing my novel again if I have had a few days away from it – it is much easier to pick up the threads if you already know what the next scene will be, or how the one you stopped writing part way through will continue.

The tutors of Creative Writing who oppose the idea of a synopsis have one main argument against it: it is restricting, they say; it puts you into a strait-jacket, and allows no scope for your imagination; and it prevents you from experiencing the delight of finding that one of your characters has 'come to life', and is doing all sorts of things you hadn't expected – even 'taking over' and leading your story off in a totally unexpected direction.

Well, all that is nonsense. The synopsis is not imposed on you from outside – it is your own work, and therefore you can change it whenever you like. If it doesn't work, or if you have a better idea, there's no reason why you shouldn't depart from it. Even if you have been lucky enough to get a commission to write your novel on the basis of a synopsis and specimen chapter, the publisher is extremely unlikely to be difficult if you have departed in some respect from your original story, especially if it has been improved as a result – unless, of course, you have altered it so drastically that the gentle romance he or she is expecting has turned into a bodice-ripper of the most sensational and ill-written sort.

As for restricting the imagination, I think those who suggest that this will happen are forgetting that the synopsis itself is built out of imagination – indeed, where else can it come from? Even if you are writing the kind of historical novel which is very firmly based on a real-life person, you will use your imagination in your portrayal and in the selection of events which make up your story. A novel is not photographic – it selects, it highlights, it manipulates characters and events to make a good story – and the setting out of a synopsis is a way of controlling those processes to the best advantage.

Those of us who do work with a tight synopsis are not deprived of the excitement of finding that one of our characters has come to life. To begin with, this can easily happen at synopsis stage. When you are working out the plan for your book, the central characters should indeed come alive in your mind, and affect the course of the story. I begin a novel by thinking about it in fairly vague terms; by the time I begin to work out a synopsis, I have some idea of where it is going and of who the main characters in it are; but when I get down to the detail of the synopsis, those characters often insist on doing things that I had not originally thought of, or refusing to follow my intentions for them; they have indeed come to life.

This can happen equally with minor characters.

But of course this is not what the anti-synopsis people mean. They are thinking of the character who comes to life while you are part way through the actual writing of the book. Well, that too has happened to me several times in the course of the novels I have written, and very welcome it has been. However, the story that I have to tell is to me of paramount importance, so when a character comes to life and starts 'taking over' and doing things I hadn't planned for him or her, I go back to my synopsis and see whether I can use this development to increase the power of the novel. I do the same if I have some brilliant idea which changes some facet of the story. Often I can work the new development in, and do so with delight. On the other hand, if it seems to me that this rebellious character, or this new twist in the tale, is going to lead the novel in a totally new direction in which I do not wish to go, then I will discard the idea or go back to the point in the material that I have already written at which the character began this 'coming to life' business, and rewrite so that I keep my storyline intact.

It could be, of course, that the character that has come to life will change the whole story radically but in a way that is preferable to your original concept. Then, I would suggest, it's back to the drawing board and the production of a new synopsis. I must say, however, that if you have spent sufficient time and effort on the original synopsis, you should be so wedded to it that you will not want to change the storyline except in minor ways.

In the end, however, the decision as to whether or not to prepare a tight synopsis, and for the most part stick to it, must be yours. There are no rules about the way to write a book – each writer must discover what works best for him or her – and many successful historical novels have been written by someone who started the story without any idea of where it was going or how it was going to end. Such people are extraordinarily gifted, and I still recommend planning for all beginners. In any case, I always have a suspicion that the begin-and-let's-see-where-it-takes-me writer does in fact have a good idea of what's going to happen in the story, but may not be aware of it because the planning has been going on in his or her subconscious.

Where to Begin

In order to start writing a synopsis you need, I think, three things: an originating spark, a central character (or sometimes characters, but usually not more than four), and a plot (which is simply another word for a story).

By 'originating spark' I mean whatever it is that first makes you want to write a story. It can be a character, or something of apparently minor significance, such as a single scene that you visualise, or a chance phrase that has come into your mind or which you have overheard, or it may be simply your desire to present a picture of people living in a different age from our .own. For my own novels, the originating spark has been in each case the background – the idea of writing a story set against a particular industry in Victorian times.

The originating spark is then developed into the bare outline of your story. For instance, you may have a desire to write a novel about an imaginary episode in the life of Henry VIII – perhaps you have visualised a scene in which a terrified young woman cowers weeping before him. That is the originating spark. You develop it by deciding that the story will be about a young woman – let's call her Lady Mary Whatshername – beautiful, intelligent, high-spirited, who has a torrid affair with Henry before eventually being thrown over in favour of Katherine Howard. Some people would call that a plot, but I would say that it is no more than an originating spark. A plot, at least in my terms, is the whole storyline, telling how Lady Mary meets Henry, how their affair develops, how he turns from her to Katherine Howard, how she reacts, plus all the other developments and sub-plots and so on.

Another way of expressing this is to say that the originating spark is what the story is to be about, not the story itself, not the plot, but the basic theme. For the historical novel, this theme will always be a dual one – what the story is about, whether it is rags-to-riches or love-conquers-all or revenge or a background or whatever, *plus* the historical setting.

You will be told by tutors of Creative Writing and in books on the subject that characters must always come before plots, and it is true. Plots develop from the characters, and their actions and reactions. Once you have found your originating spark, you will therefore need to know your central characters in some depth, and to build them up in your mind, and perhaps on paper, in the way that will be discussed later in the chapter on Characterisation. You will also begin to supply the central characters with relations, friends and acquaintances (though some of these may be added at a later stage).

By this time, your storyline may be forming, even if it is still shadowy. You will have also probably decided on the scope of your book – whether it is to be limited to a small group of people and a comparatively simple storyline, or whether it will be long and complex, with many sub-plots and a huge cast of characters. Another decision which you have probably reached by now is the time-span of your story, which may be anything from a few days to a century or more.

I would suggest that the next thing to do is to decide where the story will end – the goal to which you are driving – and when it will begin.

We shall be discussing the beginning and ending of a novel in more detail at a later stage, but for now let me simply say that you should almost certainly start just as, or just before, your central character is presented with circumstances which will change his or her life. Perhaps, if you are writing the story of Henry VIII and Lady Mary Whatshername, you will begin when Lady Mary's father announces that the family is to move to London and to become part of the Court. Ask yourself how Lady Mary reacts to this. Does she perhaps love the idea and start dreaming of attracting Henry's attention, or does she hate it because she will have to leave her childhood sweetheart behind? In that case, perhaps you will begin not with Lady Mary's father, but when she tells the young man of the bombshell her father has dropped.

As for the ending, that too will probably come after a major crisis in your central character's life – one which rounds off the story you have to tell, tying most of the threads together, and, one hopes, leaving the reader satisfied.

Once you have a beginning and an end in mind, you have to decide what goes in between. The middle, of course, is the story. There is a basic formula for almost all novels: give your central character a goal, and then put barriers in his or her way. The barriers can be physical, but more often and more effectively are caused by other people. Let us suppose for a moment that Lady Mary's great ambition is to marry Henry and become Queen of England. First, of course, she must meet the king, but her father refuses to take the family to London. How can she get there against her father's will? That is a barrier which you have created for her and which she must overcome.

Work out a credible solution to that problem, and then go on from there. How does she attract the king's attention? How does she react when he pays her attention? If her father and mother, and perhaps her childhood sweetheart, do come to London, how do they react, and do they take any action to save her from Henry's lechery? Perhaps they will do everything in their power to stop the affair, and that is another barrier for her to surmount. The nature of the barrier will depend on the characters you have built up for them – it could be that her father and mother are ambitious, and are delighted with the idea that their daughter might become the Queen of England, and it is only her sweetheart who tries to save her honour. And of course it depends on the kind of story that you want to tell.

There must be further incidents – you may introduce a villain, who does everything possible to frustrate Lady Mary (more barriers). Work out not only what the villain does, but why. There will also be other characters, including perhaps some real-life people, and historical events which may touch Lady Mary's life, and affect her in some major way.

The solution your central character finds to cope with a barrier that you put in his or her path will often lead on to the next barrier. This is why the best plots arise out of the characters, because so often the traits which lead that character to climb over the obstacle in a particular way will cause further complications.

You will also want to consider adding sub-plots. A story which concentrates on one set of circumstances only is likely to seem thin. Besides, any group of characters is bound at some time to be affected by the activities of others, and that, for your purpose, means exploring those activities and the motives behind them – in other words, creating sub-plots. One important thing to remember, however, is that your sub-plots must be knitted into the main story – they must affect the principal characters.

You might, in this story of which we are speaking, think of a sub-plot concerned, for instance, with the financial problems of Lady Mary's father.

If the climax of the book is to come with Henry throwing Mary over in favour of Katherine Howard, Katherine herself will probably have an important part to play in the story. Will she be Mary's friend, or her deadly rival? Perhaps she will be the villain of the piece. More subtly, she might be apparently Mary's dearest friend, but secretly her deadliest enemy. And is the ending to be down-beat, with Mary retreating to her country home in disgrace, or are you going to allow her to end up with the man who has truly loved her all through the story, and who is pleased to take her as his bride despite her little fling with His Majesty? In that case you will need to introduce him fairly early on in the book, and he will be more than a minor background figure throughout the story.

The more sub-plots you introduce (and the more major characters), the more complex your story will become, and it is important to interweave the various strands so that they form a whole, rather than appearing as separate incidents. Read *The Raj Quartet,* and marvel at the way Paul Scott handles so many different themes, dropping one while he concentrates on another, but never losing sight of the many characters and their stories, and yet forming them into a coherent whole.

One further thing that you must think about is the need to find opportunities to introduce dramatic scenes and conflict, without which the novel will lack pace and tension.

Until now you have probably been working all this out only in your mind, but soon you will reach the point when you want to put it down on paper. It is often very difficult to do so – there are so many strands of the story buzzing around in your head – and it's especially troublesome if you try to set it all out in chronological order. You will also probably find that you have not sorted out all the details, and will have to invent reasons for this or that development in the story. New ideas will come to you, and often out of sequence. You will frequently ask yourself, 'How can I make this happen?' Perhaps you want to engineer a rift between Henry and Lady Mary. Then you might say, 'What if she were to ask him point-blank for money for her father, which would send him into a violent rage?' or 'What if he were suddenly called away on affairs of State and she, unaware that his duties had taken him from her, were to believe that he had abandoned her?' Some of those ideas you will discard as unworkable or boring, or for some other reason, and you will go on asking yourself, 'How can I make this happen?' and 'What if . . .' until you begin to sort it all out in your mind.

When I am going through this process, I usually write longhand, and the paper is soon a mess of notes and crossings out and balloons with words in them to be inserted here or there and odd ideas which haven't yet been fitted in and people's names and reminders of research to be done. I usually then leave it for a while before trying to make sense of it all, coming back not only when my mind is, I hope, a little fresher, but also after my subconscious has had a chance to work on the various problems. At this point I don't worry too much about chronological order, being much more concerned about getting as many ideas as possible in some written form, however cryptic and jumbled they may be.

The next stage is the preparation of the synopsis itself, incorporating all my notes in the plan so that they are put in in the right place and the whole thing begins to have some kind of coherence. It is now that I begin to look for the shape of the story, making sure that the major events in it are spaced out, that the dramatic content is strong enough to carry the narrative along towards the main climax at the end of the story. Shape, with its visual connotations, is a useful word. Look at your story as though it were a line on a graph, rising and falling as the various dramatic events follow each other, as the tension increases or slackens a little. The overall shape of the line should be a gently ascending one, reaching its highest point at the final climax. You can, if you wish, divide your synopsis into chapters, and this will help you to see even more clearly the shape of the story.

It is a very good idea – indeed, it is more or less essential, especially for a historical novel – to draw up a timetable of the events in your story. This will cover such matters as the ages of your principal characters at various points, the seasons, and you should certainly also make a note of major historical happenings – wars, the accession of a new monarch, natural disasters, new laws, and the like – which will affect your characters' lives. Remember that life moved at a slower pace in bygone ages – news took far longer to reach its destination, travel was slow. And bear in mind that, although it is perfectly possible for people to fall in love and pop into bed, whether married or not, almost immediately, often the process takes much longer; equally, if your hero is to rise to the top of his profession, it will probably take him many years to do so.

A timetable will help you to make sure that if you describe events taking place on, say, a Friday and then continue by saying, 'Four days later . . .', you remember that it is now Tuesday, not Monday or Wednesday. It sounds elementary, but it is very easy to slip up on such trivial matters, and a schedule of dates and timings can be invaluable.

When to Start Writing

Don't be too eager to start writing the book itself. If you accept the idea of planning, understand that it is not something to be dashed off in a hurry. It may well take you as long to work out a synopsis as to write the text. It is a time in which you let your imagination play, and when the synopsis is first written down in a formal way, it is not necessarily finished. Leave it alone for a while. Don't even think about it, unless ideas come to you unbidden, though you may take the opportunity to do some more research. When you come back to it, see how any new ideas you may have had or which your research has thrown up will fit into it. Do everything you can to improve it, and only when you are sure that you have got it as near right as possible, begin the actual writing.

And do remember that your synopsis is not sacrosanct. It will be your guide as you write, but it can always be changed when some better way of achieving an effect occurs to you, or if a character suddenly comes to life (provided that you remain faithful to the book you set out to produce in the first place).

The Title

Some writers find it essential to decide on the title of the novel before they begin writing. They find that having a title helps the whole thing to come alive for them, and in a strange way spurs them on to write the book. If you are such a writer, then the decision comes at planning time (indeed, the title may be the originating spark), and it is worth spending quite a lot of time on it until you get something which really satisfies you. Do not worry, on the other hand, if you don't want to think about a title until you have finished the book, when it is possible that you will find it easier to settle on exactly the right wording.

Whenever it is that you choose your title, try to pick something which is fully relevant to your story, and which seems to have a ring to it. Familiar quotations are often a source of titles, but beware of choosing something which is either too hackneyed or which may have connotations which do not fit your particular novel. If the title also suggests the period, that is perhaps a bonus, but there is no need to worry on this score unduly. Finally, I would like to suggest, although you can probably quote examples of successful books which do not follow this advice, that you try to avoid the kind of obscure title which gives no hint at all of what kind of book it is.

3

CHARACTERISATION

The portrayal of interesting characters in considerable depth is the most important aspect of any novel. We can do without an exciting story, we can do without detailed descriptions of the age or of the scenery, we can do without a whole number of things, but we cannot do without characters who will come alive for us as we turn the pages of the book, and in whose actions, reactions, emotions and ambitions we become deeply involved. Human beings are undoubtedly the most interesting things in the world to other human beings, especially to readers of novels.

Moreover, it is out of the characters that your story develops. They are the force which makes things happen. They cause certain events in the novel to occur, or if they are affected by what happens outside themselves, their reactions lead on to other situations.

It is therefore essential that you should know your characters as thoroughly as you know yourself before you even begin to write about them. Many tutors of Creative Writing advise you to write down all the essential information in list form, starting with your principal characters. The details will include: age, height, weight, physical appearance, colouring, address, occupation, financial situation, parentage, upbringing, education, past history, intelligence, attitude to life, nature, opinion of self, relationships with others, reactions of others to the character, and anything else you can think of which may be relevant. This exercise is not to be done casually – you must see the character in your mind, you must work out the details so that you build up a really full picture. If you do this successfully, then you will know immediately how your character will react to any situation, you will be able to hear what he or she says, and you will see the effect that he or she has on others.

When you have done this for your main characters, go on to the less important ones, perhaps with not quite so much detail, but still with sufficient for you to be sure that you really know them. It is worth noting at this point that the driving force behind the events of the novel is not always the main character. To explain what I mean by this, think of *Macbeth* – Macbeth himself is undoubtedly the central figure in the drama, but it is Lady Macbeth who causes it all to happen. If you have such a character in your story – one who, as it were, controls the destiny of your hero or heroine – you must certainly explore that person in great depth.

Although I myself give this advice to my students, I have to admit that I do not always follow it to the extent of writing down everything about my characters. But I do work out all the details mentally, usually at the stage when I am trying to put together my synopsis, and I take sufficient time over it and think about the characters so much that they become fully real to me. Thinking is indeed part of writing.

To begin with, you will mould your characters to fit the story that you want to tell, but you will find that they also mould the story. While you are thinking about them (or later when you are writing about them) they may well come to life, assume characteristics that you have not expected and do things that you had not originally envisaged. I have discussed in the chapter on Planning how you should deal with this exciting situation.

It is important not only to *know* your characters, but to *understand* them. One of them, for instance, may be the implacable enemy of your hero or heroine – a thoroughly unpleasant person whom you want your readers to hate. But to present such a character successfully, you *must* know why he or she acts in that way, what has caused the viciousness, and whether it is, as it were, a temporary aberration or whether it is a deep-rooted part of the character's nature. In short, you must understand and sympathise with such people, even if you don't like what they do. To take another example, you might have a scene in your book when one character is putting forward a point of view which you do not hold yourself – perhaps someone is arguing with Henry VIII against the Disestablishment of the Church, which in your view was A Good Thing – nevertheless, you must understand the arguments against the idea, and put them forward, through your character, with as much conviction and understanding as though you believed them yourself.

The Main Character

Do make sure that you like your central character. If you don't like him or her, how can you expect your readers to do so? One of your main aims should be to get readers to identify with your hero or heroine, and they cannot do so if the character is one whose point of view they cannot sympathise with or understand.

In general, although it may sound as though you will be creating a stereotype, your main character should be admirable, and possess the qualities of virtues, courage and amiability. A sense of humour is also invaluable, and is an antidote to pomposity or priggishness. Your hero or heroine should have great strength of character (or should acquire it in the course of the book), and should be ready to fight for what he or she wants, and to face adversity with determination.

At the same time, don't let him or her become an impossible paragon. We all have failings, and we like other people to have them too. So even heroes and heroines sometimes get out of bed on the wrong side, they too can snap at people and say things they don't mean and later regret. And, as we all do, they tell lies (which, incidentally, may lead to all kinds of interesting complications which will help to carry your plot along).

One of the easiest ways of arousing your readers' sympathies for your hero or heroine is to make him, or her, the victim of some injustice, which will eventually, we hope, be put right. And it is very helpful to have a villain – someone who, for much of the book, thwarts your main character and erects barriers in his or her path. But just as no one is perfect and the hero or heroine, however admirable and likeable, should have some weaknesses, so your villain should have one or two redeeming features, since no one is all bad – perhaps he or she loves his or her spouse, or has an unswerving loyalty to the King, or is kind to children.

The Female Central Character

Attitudes towards women have changed very considerably in the late twentieth century. Before then, primarily as a result of Jewish, Christian and Islamic teachings, women were regarded as inferior to men, and despite a few notable exceptions such as Boadicea, Elizabeth I and Florence Nightingale, were expected to restrict themselves to marriage, the bearing of children, and domestic chores, with perhaps, if they had sufficient leisure, a little needlework, or a dabbling in watercolours to pass their time. If they were peasants, they might work alongside their menfolk in the fields, but they were always subservient to men, and, whatever their social backgrounds, to have had pronounced opinions or any independence meant that they were odd (and in some centuries might well have been accused of witchcraft). Up to the nineteenth century, the concept of marrying for love was barely known – marriages were arranged by parents, and although men had some degree of choice, the young woman's feelings were rarely taken into account.

Since you are writing for a modern audience to whom these attitudes may be anathema, especially as the majority of historical novel readers are women, it is sensible, if you have a female as the main character, to make her a rebel – a woman who wants a career rather than cow-like domesticity, or who refuses to accept as her husband the man her parents have chosen for her, a female worker who believes that labour is not only dignified, but should be fairly rewarded, an ambitious woman who aspires to wealth and power. Be aware, however, that such people were unusual in their times, and remember that if you want to give them a twentieth-century outlook, you must temper it by the context of the period in which they live. This is not to say that they cannot be strong, determined characters, but simply that they themselves must understand that they are rebels, and that the achievement of their ambitions should be feasible.

Putting the Characters on the Page

The work of getting to know your characters is rather like research – indeed, it is a form of it. As we shall see later in the chapter on Research, one of the questions you will face is how you will tell your readers all that you have learnt. The presentation of the people in your book is a similar problem.

You can, of course, go into a long description as soon as the character is introduced, setting down all the relevant information, but this may well prove indigestible, so that your readers will not take it all in. Besides which, it will hold up the story when you should probably be getting on with the action in the form of a scene. Rather than a long character study and physical description, it is much better to let everything come out a little more gradually. Characters are in any case built more effectively by showing their actions and their reactions to events and other characters in the story, and by the reaction of those other characters to them. You can also reveal character in the way your people dress – in the latest fashion or in out-of-date clothes, sloppily or smartly. Or in the way they keep their homes – describe a room, and you have a picture of its owner.

As with research, while you should know everything possible about the subject or the character, you may not need to give all the information to the reader, and one of the advantages of not revealing everything is that your readers will be able to work things out for themselves, which is something that they like to do. Never ever tell the reader that a character is bitchy, or courageous, or whatever it may be – make a scene of it, and let the reader see it for himself, or herself.

Don't forget thoughts. The novelist has the great advantage of being able to let the reader see what various characters are thinking, which may often be in contrast to what they say or do. At the same time, beware of the fact that most of us nowadays have a smattering of psychology. Let your characters analyse their own motives and those of others, by all means, but remember that psychology is a very recent science, and its terms are to be avoided because of their anachronistic qualities – no one, for instance, in the sixteenth century would talk of 'an inferiority complex'.

You must also allow your main characters to develop. By the end of the book they should be changed in some way – older and wiser, perhaps, or fulfilled, or humbled, and this must be a gradual process which continues throughout the book. The story, as has already been said, grows out of the characters, and the characters must grow with it. Although your characters should change in this way, never let them behave totally out of character. If the people in your story have become fully real to you, a little warning bell will probably sound in your head if you allow them to do or say something which does not fit in with all that you know of them. Use the 'would he really?' test – ask yourself 'would he really do that?', 'would she really say that?'. The mere fact of asking the questions will probably indicate that he or she wouldn't.

Look at the way successful authors put their characters on the page and let them develop. William Horwood, the author of *The Duncton Trilogy* and of many other fine novels, including the splendid *Skallagrigg,* suggests as first-class examples of characterisation Mrs Moore in *A Passage to India* by E. M. Forster, the central character in de Maupassant's *Boule de Suif,* or The Rev. Septimus Harding in *The Warden* by Anthony Trollope.

Historical Personages

If the characters in your novel are people who actually lived, a lot of your work in building up their picture has already been done for you. If, for instance, Henry VIII plays a major part in the story, you probably already know a fair amount about him. You will have a rough idea of what he looked like, what sort of man he was, and you can make a guess at how he would react to any given situation. However, your image of him, and that of your readers, may in fact be rather sketchy, based on a few half-remembered details from history lessons at school, the fact that he had six wives, plus such film performances as that of Charles Laugh ton and Robert Shaw. You will need to know a great deal more, and will clearly need to read as much about him as possible. The same applies, of course, to minor characters in the story if they were real-life persons. Look at the illustrations in biographies and histories – most of them will reproduce portraits of many of the people in whom you are interested, and a great deal can be gleaned from the pictures about their characters as well as their physical appearance. Don't restrict yourself to biographies, but find out about the whole background of history at the time in question.

If you are using historical personages, to what extent can you manipulate them for the purposes of your story? Obviously you cannot change historical facts, but to some extent you can bend them, and you can certainly invent attitudes and happenings, especially for lesser-known historical characters. The dialogue that you give your characters will necessarily be imaginative. The important point is that in all these expeditions into fictional territories, you should know enough about the characters concerned to feel reasonably sure that whatever you give them to do or to say is based on that knowledge – it is within their characters, and might have happened in the circumstances which you are describing.

Imaginary Characters

Where do fictional characters come from? Partly from observation – people we know and others that we observe merely from a distance, can all provide us with characters, although most novelists rarely take a character direct from life, but build up an amalgam, with a little bit from that person, something else from another, and so on.

However, most fictional characters come, I believe, from within the author. Paul Horgan, the American who wrote *A Distant Trumpet,* which I believe to be one of the finest of historical novels, says: 'I am everyone in my novel. If this were not so, no one in my novel would have a chance to ring true, even as I work to make each character an individual, different from the rest.'

In my own novels the same is true. All my characters are me – me as I am, me as I would like to be, me as I despise myself, me in many different facets.

Most novelists are like Walter Mitty, and easily imagine themselves into different persona and different situations. We all have the same basic emotions and instincts – buried beneath the surface there is a streak of violence in the mildest of old ladies, and somewhere in his nature the most aggressively butch male has an element of femininity. Novelists use not only those parts of their natures which are familiar to themselves and their friends, but also dredge up those aspects of themselves which are normally hidden, and which they may not even know are there, buried deep in the subconscious. In many ways we may seem quite different from people of bygone times, but in fact the differences are superficial, because they were human just as we are. It is therefore easily possible for you, madam, with a little effort, to imagine yourself into the person of Henry VIII, just as it is possible for me to become Lady Mary Whatshername. We may not be quite so successful with the portrayal of members of the opposite sex as we are with our own, but we can make a good shot at it. If we fail, it is usually because we have not done sufficient work in building up in our minds the character concerned.

Naming the Characters

Of course you cannot tamper with the names of historical personages who actually existed. Katherine Howard has to remain Katherine Howard, although there is nothing to stop you deciding that in private King Henry always referred to her as Katie (or even as Rosamund, or Celia, if you like, on the grounds that there were too many Katherines in his life).

When it comes to imaginary characters, you will have to choose their names with care. Firstly, make sure that they are in period. Secondly, choose names that seem to you to suit the characters, although you will probably avoid going as far as some of Restoration dramatists who named the people in their plays to reflect their characteristics – Squire Sullen, Lady Bountiful, Sir Jasper Fidget. Thirdly, try not to select names which will confuse the reader by their similarity.

On the last point, you may find it useful to follow my own practice. When I am deciding on my characters' names, I make three lists, first writing down the letters of the alphabet for each. The first list is for the first names of the female characters, the second for the first names of the males, and the third for surnames. I then set out, for each of the lists, to choose names which have a different initial letter; if I cannot entirely manage that, at least I try not to have more than two names with the same initial, and certainly never for two major characters. I also try to select names which have a differing number of syllables – Jane, Susan, Elizabeth, for example. You may feel that this is a finicky and laborious process, but I believe that easily distinguishable names help the reader to keep the characters separated in his or her mind, and especially if your novel is long and complex, this may be very important.

4

RESEARCH

To write a historical novel you do not have to be already expert in the historical background. It will certainly help if you are, but it is not by any means essential. However, you will need to become expert.

Most of us have a considerable amount of knowledge of the past tucked away in our minds – facts we learned at school, details that we have picked up from reading other people's books, and, in recent times, all that has been recreated before our very eyes in costume dramas on the television. You are almost certain to find, however, that, while some simple facts are clear enough to you – such as, for example, the date of the Armada, or perhaps that rabbits were unknown in England before the Norman Conquest – much of the information you have stored away is an awful jumble.

It contains half-truths and confusions, and it is certainly not enough for you to consider yourself an expert.

However, you need not despair. You can find out all you need to know by research.

You will almost certainly discover that you have a considerable amount of work to do. Even though the material to be found in history books concerning your chosen period may not have much to do with your story, you need to know about it. And apart from being familiar with kings and queens and wars and laws and all the other things which greatly affected the course of history, you must have a vast amount of additional knowledge – about social conditions, moral conventions, attitudes to women, education, working practices, and a host of other matters, such as housing, transport, money, food and drink and the times of day at which meals were consumed, names, clothing, heating and lighting, pastimes, the physical geography of the country at the time, and so on and so forth.

Research is concerned not merely with major events and their influence, but with little things too – with what might be called 'period detail'. What was the ink made from which children used when writing the alphabet in their hornbooks? How often were the rushes on the floor of a medieval castle changed? You need to know everything. Always check your facts. Even the things you believe you know already need to be verified.

Your aim should be to think yourself into your period so thoroughly that you will feel yourself actually a part of it as you write. Much of the material you unearth will not appear in your novel (a point which will be discussed in the chapter on How to Tell the Story), but you will not be able to write convincingly about the period unless you have the knowledge in the back of your mind. You will also be able to avoid the disaster of an anachronism. The most famous literary anachronism is the striking clock which appears in *Julius Caesar* long before such instruments were invented; but, unlike the contemporary writer, Shakespeare is perhaps allowed the occasional slip.

It all sounds formidable, and perhaps it is, but the majority of historical novelists find that research is an immensely pleasurable part of their work. Moreover, although it may be time-consuming, it is comparatively easy to find sources of information.

Where do you start? You could begin by making a list of all the things you want to know. It will probably be an enormous list, but don't be discouraged. As you start looking for information, you will find that great rivers of it come flowing in, and you will soon reduce the list to a much smaller one of the matters which are difficult to unearth. Even they can be discovered, given patience and application.

But where do you look? Almost anywhere.

The Internet is a good starting place – but beware, accuracy is not always to hand. It is all too easy for people to 'post' articles, opinions and views without proper research on their part. Many sites that claim to be the last word on a subject are often inaccurate. To some extent this can be ameliorated by selecting only those sites known to have a reputation for accuracy – very often the sites academics themselves use. Look at the relevant department pages within top university sites. These often give links to other reference sites that have been approved as suitable research vehicles by professors who are knowledgeable in their fields.

A word of caution, however; the internet will not enable you to do more than find references to particular detail. It cannot be used as a 'lazy' way of conducting research. It is simply a tool at your disposal, albeit a decidedly useful tool, which is a good point of reference. You will fall short if, for instance, you have decided to write an American 'Civil War' novel without prior knowledge and then simply read a few quickly obtained articles on your screen and, after a day or two's perusing, believe you know enough to start writing. You don't! The atmosphere of the period will elude you and your story – it will miss a vital ingredient that will make it appear threadbare to the reader. You don't require a huge amount of detail to create the right atmosphere – the last thing needed is for your story to become a historical synopsis – it is only when you have mastered the whole to a reasonable level that you are able to pick out a couple of relevant facts that bring your novel to life. So beware of too much reliance on armchair internet research!

An alternative place to begin is reading school history text books, which will provide you with some basic and easily digested facts. From there you could move on to history books which deal with your particular period, and, especially if one of your main characters is a historical figure, biographies. Don't be contented with just one book on the subject, but read as widely as possible the histories available for you chosen area. A point to remember is that detail is required – many books of social history cover a single century or period, and may therefore give you much more than a general overview of main events.

Don't neglect authors who were writing at the time you are interested in. Their books can immerse you in a period more effectively than any other method. Think of the vast amount of information to be gleaned from Dickens, for example. And what a detailed picture Jane Austen gives of the lives of the moderately well-to-do during the Regency period. Of course you will not confine yourself to fiction – contemporary plays, biographies, books of essays, factual accounts, diaries (Pepys and Evelyn, for example), all kinds of documents, will all give you an entry into the life of past ages. There are dozens of other sources for your background material and research methods.

Something else that you can do is to go to your Public Library. Librarians are experts in the retrieval of knowledge, and are invariably willing to spend a great deal of time and effort in finding books which will answer your problems – indeed, there seems to be nothing which gives a librarian more pleasure than to be confronted by an author asking where certain information is to be found. You will not be restricted to the books that happen to be in the particular library that you visit – the librarian will scour the files and obtain books for you from other libraries all over the country, and even from abroad.

If you need some specialist information, you can follow the same kind of programme that I have used in respect of the industrial background when writing my own novels. I begin always by consulting an ancient edition of the *Encyclopaedia Britannica* which I am lucky enough to possess. In several cases it has given me an essential piece of information which has provided a starting point. In the case of *Mario's Vineyard,* for instance, it was the *Britannica* which told me about phylloxera, which became the first motive for all Mario's subsequent adventures, and for *The Silk Maker* it led me to investigate the enormous success of the silk crepe manufacturing industry in the second half of the nineteenth century.

Next I go to the local library, where the librarian will almost always find a number of books which help me. Very often there will be one key volume which I can mine for an enormous amount of detail.

I always try to visit the area about which I am writing. Although the novels are set a hundred years or more ago, it is comparatively easy to obliterate mentally the high-rise buildings, and the television aerials, and anything else which belongs to a later period than the one I am writing about. I can then visualise the various localities as they must have been in earlier times. I always take special note of the surrounding countryside, and find out from local sources how it has changed – the woods that have been cut down, the ponds that have been filled in, and so on. Above all I try to soak up the atmosphere of the place.

While in the area I visit the local museums and trade centres. In such places you can usually find someone who knows a great deal about the subject you are interested in, and such experts are almost always willing to pass their knowledge on. One of the facts which helps research of any kind is that most people are always ready to talk about their work, their pet interests, their expertise. Never be afraid to ask an expert's advice, or worry about taking up his or her time – provided your interest is genuine, the only problem with such people usually is to stop them talking.

All this, of course, is in addition to the general research I have done into the social background of my characters, life in general in the period concerned, and the major historical events, which, even if my characters are not directly concerned, cannot be ignored.

There are two other things with which I always take particular care. One is the clothes that my characters will wear. The description of clothes is a particularly graphic way of conveying a sense of period, but that is not the only reason for my interest in them. I believe that people's attitudes are very much affected by their dress, and not only by the outer clothing, but by what they wear underneath. An obvious example is the corset, and the restriction of physical movement that it causes, which is often reflected in the wearer's general behaviour. If you have any doubts about this, think of the difference in your own mental attitude if you are slopping about in old comfortable clothes or dressed up to the nines for some formal affair. A good book on costume will give you a great deal of useful information, including the colours which were fashionable at given times.

My second obsession is with names. I always spend

time with my greatly treasured copy of *The Guinness Book of Names* which tells me which names were fashionable at various periods of history, and which were rare, or even completely unknown, at the time.

Just as there are specialist books on costume and names, there are others on transport through the ages, and buildings, food, etiquette, the cost of living, and so on. The store of recorded knowledge about the past is huge, and almost everything that you could ever want to know can be found in a book somewhere.

However hard all this may sound it is worthwhile. You will write with authority, and it will give you confidence to know that all the details in your story are correct. Moreover, you will be able to counter effectively anyone, including a knowledgeable copy-editor, who challenges you on a particular point. And, of course, it becomes easier if you write other novels set in the same period, because you will already have much of the background knowledge, and will need to research for specialised information only.

The Cost of Research

Writing is not a particularly costly business – you may need to lash out on a word processor (or be prepared to pay someone to type your books for you), but otherwise you will little to buy You may later have to spend quite a lot in postage as you send your typescript off to potential publishers, if they do not accept submissions by email, but even that is not going to drain most people's bank accounts too drastically.

Research, on the other hand, can be expensive, especially if it involves travel. If you can afford it, that's fine; if not, then perhaps you could combine a holiday with travel to the place you want to research; if even that is impossible, then you will have to rely on books. Fortunately, it is not too difficult for most people to get to a Public Library, and then the riches of the written word are available to you.

It is even better, of course, especially if you want to make a career of writing historical novels, to build up your own library of reference books. This could be a very expensive business, but you might be able to overcome this problem by being ready with the name of a book the next time someone asks what you want for Christmas or your birthday. I think you probably do need some basic books – a basic history of whichever country your books are to be set in, a social history, a costume book, and so on. And if you find in the library a key book for the novel you are writing, it is well worth buying your own copy if you can.

Do remember, by the way, that any expenses you incur in the writing of a book can, for tax purposes, be set against your earnings from it when it is published.

When to do the Research

How much of all the research must be done before you begin writing? A large part of it! Certainly you need to have steeped yourself in your particular period before you begin, and you will probably want to know as much as possible about all the events which will affect the daily lives of your characters. But I think that most historical novelists find that research is a more or less continuous business. As the story advances, you will find that you need this or that piece of information which has so far escaped you. The late John Creasey used to say, 'Write first, research later,' but he was writing contemporary crime stories and thrillers, and I think he was really talking about minor things, such as which number bus you would catch to get from A to B, or how much beer costs in a bar. Little details of that sort can certainly be filled in at a later stage, but in general the more research you do in advance, the easier the writing of the story will be.

Besides, as I say, you cannot always anticipate every bit of information that you will need, and sometimes you will feel that you cannot continue with the writing, despite John Creasey, until you have discovered a certain detail. Yet another thing which can happen is that in searching for one such piece of information you discover something else which may have a major effect on your story. So the answer is to keep at it.

Another good reason for doing the larger part of your research, before you even begin to write the synopsis, is that it can sometimes be immensely useful in the actual plotting of your story. I have already mentioned the effect that my discovery of phylloxera had when I was writing *Mario's Vineyard.* In fact, the date at which I began the story was determined by the little phylloxera insect, because it arrived in Italy in 1878, and so, because of the effect it had on my vine-growing family, that was when the book opened. Another example came later in that novel. I wanted to dispose of one of my characters; I had already despatched a number of people with various diseases, and I wanted a different kind of death for this person, if only for the sake of variety; I suddenly realised that in the narrative I had reached 1906, so I sent the poor man off to San Francisco (naturally finding a good reason why he should go there) on 17th April, the night before the earthquake, and that was the end of him. I did not have to research the fact that the earthquake took place in 1906 – that was already in the jumble of more or less useless information at the back of my mind. I did, however, need to check the actual day and then to research exactly what happened in some detail, so that the whole episode could be as authentic as possible.

One problem that you may find is that historical dates do not always fit conveniently into your story. In my novel, *The Cast Iron Man*, the Boer War could not go unnoticed, and indeed it affected one of the characters quite drastically (another case of me playing God and sending the person concerned off to be killed). Now, the Boer War began in 1899, and I really didn't want it to do so, because it didn't fit well into the time-span between various other happenings in the novel. Of course, there was no way that I could rearrange the start of the Boer War, so I had to rejig the other dates in the story which concerned fictional events.

Of course, you can never alter history. You may bend it a little by the introduction of fictional characters, or the emphasis you put on events, but you can't change dates and you can't alter the kind of facts which everyone knows. You might write a novel about Elizabeth I in which you suggest that she was anything but a Virgin Queen, and you might get away with it because most of us suspect that she may well have been a bit of a lass, but you can't show her as weak and vacillating, or alter the fact that she came to the throne at the age of twenty-five in 1558. Even in small things, it is advisable not to follow the example of so many film-makers who think nothing of distorting history in order to make a more dramatic point. Always be as accurate as you possibly can.

What do you do if some piece of research which seems vital for your story stubbornly refuses to unearth itself? Well, you probably invent. You use your imagination. But it is informed, intelligent imagination. It comes, or should, from the deep knowledge of the period with which your research has endowed you, and because of what you know of the context in which this particular thing appears, it is likely to be a really educated guess. It is, naturally, better to go on searching until you find the required evidence, but if you fall back on invention, at least you should be able to say, 'This is the way it must have been – or if it wasn't, then it jolly well should have been.'

5

HOW TO TELL THE STORY

The Focus of Attention

Your first concern should be to decide on the 'focus of attention', a term which tutors of Creative Writing use when they are talking about the viewpoint from which the story will be told.

You can use the first person to tell your story. It is a technique which has some advantages. It is very immediate, and it is very easy to engage the sympathies of your readers, and to allow them to identify with the T who is telling the story. The main problem is that the first person narrator can only relate what he or she knows, and must be present at every scene in the book. He or she can never get inside the mind of another character, except by guesswork, and if information which is unknown to this narrator has to be conveyed, it can only be done by another character telling him or her about it, or perhaps if he or she reads an account of whatever it may be. This means, sometimes, that a scene which should be told in action has to become narration, which is a pity. Incidentally, the technique is only successful if the first person narrator is the principal character in the story – it just doesn't work if the 'I' of the story is simply an observer, recording what happens, but not really participating in the events.

The second possibility is to take the God's-eye-view, in which the narrative is told in the third person. Using this technique the author is all-seeing, and can reveal not only the actions and speech of all the characters, but also all their thoughts and motives, focusing now on this person and now on that. It is perhaps the easiest way of telling a complex story, but it has the disadvantage that it almost always makes the characters seem somewhat remote, as though they were specimens under the microscope, and it is much more difficult for the reader to identify with them, simply because the focus constantly switches from one character to another.

The approach which is most often used and is usually more successful than the others, is for the narration to be in the third person, but the focus of attention to be on the principal character only. The story is focused on this character throughout, but the author has the ability to convey information about other characters which would be very difficult to do if the narrative were presented in the first person. For instance: 'As she pleaded with him, Mary kept her eyes on his. She could not detect any change in their expression, so she remained unaware that he had already dismissed Edgar from the Court.'

There are some variations which can be used within this approach. You may have more than one main character, and may turn the attention on to each of them in turn. Or you may wish to switch occasionally to a scene in which the main character does not appear, in which case the focus of attention will be on the principal character in that episode. The one thing that you must never do is to switch viewpoints in the middle of a scene – readers find it very confusing when this happens, not knowing on which character they are supposed to be concentrating.

At the same time, it is possible sometimes to break this

last rule, and to combine both the single-character focus with minor use of the God's-eye-view, but it has to be done with great care. At the beginning of my novel, *The Silk Maker*, the focus of attention is very firmly settled on the main character, Richard, who at that point is a boy of nine; nevertheless, in the course of this opening scene, more than once I allow the reader to see briefly into the mind of a minor character, Mrs Harcourt, which Richard could not do. I think it works, because the reader is aware (or should be, at least subconsciously) that this is merely a momentary shift away from Richard, and, moreover, that he is continuing to watch what is happening. Perhaps it would have been better if I had rewritten it so that the whole scene was seen from Richard's viewpoint.

To show what I mean, let us take part of one paragraph: 'Her [Mrs Harcourt's] gaze settled on the dozen or so books which stood on the mantelshelf, and she sniffed in disapproval. Books! A family like the Goodwins had no business with books – except, of course, the Bible.'

That could have been written like this: 'Richard saw that she was looking at the dozen or so books which stood on the mantelshelf. She sniffed. He knew what she was thinking – that a family like his had no business with books, though no doubt she would not have condemned them for possessing a Bible.'

It might indeed have been better. So why didn't I do it? Because I did not believe that Richard at the age of nine would have understood what was in Mrs Harcourt's mind. I could have cut her thoughts entirely, but their inclusion allowed me to define her character more clearly, and to get over some information which I wanted the reader to have.

So a clear-cut focus of attention is not always easy to achieve, but you must try not to break the rules for maintaining it unless you really have to.

Action or Narration

Action, in this context, does not necessarily mean physical action, or even tension. It means that your readers see the scene actually taking place before their eyes, often with much use of dialogue. In narration, on the other hand, you simply tell your readers what has happened. Here is an action scene, consisting mainly of dialogue, which shows two characters quarrelling:

> 'What will you wear when you meet the King?' her mother asked.
>
> 'My new green velvet gown,' Mary replied quietly, eager to avoid the argument which she felt sure would follow.
>
> 'You will not!'
>
> 'Why not?'
>
> 'Because it is shameless. That bodice is so low-cut and so tight-fitting that it reveals ... it reveals . . . No well-born lady could wear a dress like that.'
>
> Mary tried to restrain her temper. 'Oh, mother! 'Tis the latest fashion. All the ladies at the Court dress in that style. If you think my dress is shameless, you should see what Katherine Howard wears. They say the King likes nothing better than for a woman to show a fine pair of breasts!'
>
> 'Be silent! Now you are talking like a whore!'

And so on, until the quarrel ends with Mary flying from the room in angry tears. In narration, the whole scene would be very briefly covered: 'Mary and her mother quarrelled bitterly over the dress that Mary wanted to wear for her first meeting with the King. Her mother told her that the new green velvet gown was shameless, and their argument ended with Mary running from the room in tears.'

You may not think much of either passage, but you will surely agree that the action scene has more interest and life than the narrative.

Action is always preferable to narration, at least for all the crucial points of the story. When working out the shape of your novel, you should have in it a number of highpoints; points at which something important happens – a quarrel, a declaration of love, the erection or the surmounting of a barrier in the central character's way; there are many possibilities. Each of them should be presented in action, rather than narration. Make a scene of it, whenever you can. Don't let important things happen off-stage, as it were. Bring them in front of your readers' eyes.

There is, of course, a time and a place for narration. If you use action throughout, the high spots will lose some of their effect, and moreover there may be some information which you need to give the reader which is essential but not in any way dramatic, or capable of being dramatized. For these you use narration. It is the link between the action scenes of the high spots. For instance, let us suppose that Lady Mary has a disagreement with Henry (the action of which we see), which ends with him sending her home from Court, apparently indefinitely. The story might then continue with narration:

That spring seemed endless to Mary. The weather was fine and warm, and there were primroses in abundance and the trees were bursting into leaf, and the whole world seemed to be rejoicing. In the Manor House all was happy bustle, and in the fields the peasants sang as they toiled.

For Mary, however, the days were leaden. Her mother found needlework for her to do, and her father sometimes attempted to converse with her, but nothing held her attention for long. Even at Edgar's invitations to come riding she would merely shake her head. She sat for long hours by the window of her room, the sewing neglected on her lap, gazing into the distance, but seeing nothing of the hills and vales of Derbyshire, dreaming always of Henry, the King, her lover.

And so on, until the messenger arrives to summon her back to Court, and it is there that we next see her, in an action scene as Henry welcomes her back.

Suspense and Cliff-hangers

Any good story will have plenty of conflict in it – conflict between various characters, conflict in the central character's attempts to reach a given goal, conflicts within the characters themselves. It is these conflicts which provide your story with suspense, and keep it moving. The term 'suspense' is simply another way of saying that your readers want to know what happens next. This, of course, is one of the purposes of the barriers which you erect between your central character and his or her aims. Each time you put in a barrier, if you have done it effectively, and if your readers have sympathy with the character, they will be wondering how he or she is to overcome the barrier, or escape from the predicament in which he or she has landed.

Try not to let your story be too straightforward – let the plot twist and turn. And surprise the reader if you can. Provided that it is credible and within character, you can sometimes lead the reader to expect something entirely different from what actually happens. For instance, after that example of narration given above, I suggested that a messenger might arrive summoning Mary back to court. Perhaps it is a brief message, which reveals little, but could easily be an eager lover's call for her return. Mary sets off for London in the happiest of spirits, but when she arrives, to her astonishment (and, we hope that of the reader), she finds that Henry is even angrier with her than he was before (perhaps Katherine Howard has been maligning her in her absence). Not only is the reader surprised, but he or she will wonder what will happen next – how will Mary get out of this situation?

Although you may need at times to insert various hints of what is to come later in the book (see 'Little Clouds' below), try not to tell the reader too much in advance. Be fair – don't surprise him or her with, for instance, the sudden revelation near the end of the novel that Mary has a twin sister who has been masquerading as Mary – but keep some information back so as to create suspense and surprise.

On the other hand, there are some occasions when to reveal certain facts in your story can create dramatic irony, which is often a good device for adding to suspense. Dramatic irony is the term used when the audience at a play (or the reader of a book) knows something which one of the characters does not. For instance, if the example of narration above were preceded by a scene in which Katherine Howard told Henry that Mary had been disloyal to him, and Henry said that Mary would pay for it, we are then in a situation of dramatic irony when Mary gets the message to return to London. She thinks she is going back to her lover's arms, while the reader knows that she's in for trouble. And how is she going to get out of it?

Cliff-hangers are yet another device for creating suspense. Usually they come at the end of chapters, and that is certainly their most effective position. Each episode finishes with the beginning of a new situation or a crisis, and the idea is to hook the listeners so that they all tune in next day to find out what happened. Put a cliff-hanger at the end of your chapter (perhaps when Mary arrives back at court, and goes in to see Henry he has a face like thunder – end of chapter. What will happen next? That's a cliff-hanger). The suspense created by a cliff-hanger can sometimes be increased, if your story is a fairly complex one, by switching to a different situation for the next chapter, so that the reader has to wait for the chapter after that to hear how poor Mary got on.

'Little Clouds'

I mentioned above the need occasionally to give hints of what is to happen later in your story. I like to call these hints 'little clouds' (a reference to the Biblical story of Elijah's servant who spoke of a little cloud no bigger than a man's hand, which later turned into a full-scale storm). Little clouds are rather like clues in a detective story. As an example, in my novel, *The Silk Maker,* I wanted Frances, the sister of my hero, Richard, eventually to become a designer of fabrics; I could have interested her in this work from the beginning, but I wanted it to be something of a surprise to the reader, yet at the same time something that might have been expected. I therefore dropped in, fairly early in the book, a little cloud in the form of a comment about the talent Frances had for painting. The point was not emphasised in any way, but it was, I hope, sufficient for the reader to note, and to say, when Frances later became a fabric designer, 'Ah, yes. I remember she was something of an artist.'

Here is another example. You may remember that in the chapter on Planning I suggested at one point that Katherine Howard might appear to be Lady Mary Whatshername's dearest friend, yet is in fact her enemy. You could insert a brief scene near the beginning of the book in which Katherine, talking to another lady of the Court, expresses her dislike of Lady Mary. For the next several chapters Katherine is charming and kind to Lady Mary, but readers will remember that little scene, and when Mary later discovers Katherine's true feelings, will be prepared for the surprise.

Readers are very good at picking up small points of that sort, even when you insert them, as you should, quite subtly, so be careful that you don't put in any little clouds which you're not going to make use of later.

Getting on with the Story

You must keep your narrative moving along. Don't indulge in long descriptions or passages where nothing significant happens. Get on with the important parts of the story, and move as quickly as you can from one high spot to the next.

You do not need to give every detail of some major historical event, but only those parts of it which affect your characters – you are not writing a history, which takes the broad view, but a novel in which individuals and their emotions and reactions are important. Equally, you do not need to tell your readers about minor matters which they will take for granted – for instance, you don't have to spell out the fact that your heroine goes to her virginal bed and gets up in the morning each day (unless some startling happening, which is part of your story, occurs at the moment in question). A novel is like a good painting, rather than like a photograph: the camera reproduces every detail of its subject with great accuracy, but even in a faithful canvas the artist selects what he or she wants you to see, colours it with his or her own vision of what is there, and allows parts of the subject to fade into the background, or even eliminates them altogether, while other parts may be highlighted in a way that the photograph would not do.

Never stop to explain, except perhaps to clarify some period term (and even that should, where possible, be comprehensible from the context). If the reader does not understand what is going on (unless, of course, you are deliberately creating a confusing situation which will resolve itself later in the book), then you have failed. Most readers are intelligent beings, and have become trained in working things out for themselves as they read, so while you should not take their knowledge for granted, you should never underrate their ability to put two and two together and make five, or a great deal more. They will pick up 'little clouds', they will understand from well-written scenes and dialogue the way your characters feel at the time, they will understand the irony in your juxtaposition, for instance, of a scene depicting the Court and its high-life with another scene showing the poverty of the common people. Look at *The Tailor of Gloucester,* which might be described as a historical story for children, and note that Beatrix Potter never says in so many words that the mice sewed the Mayor's new coat – she does not underestimate the intelligence of her small readers, leaving them to deduce it for themselves.

Don't put in too many minor characters who have no real part to play in your story, and if you must mention, for instance, a servant who appears at one point in the story and for the most minor of reasons, then don't name that servant. To give a character a name has the same effect as a 'little cloud' – your reader immediately becomes interested in the person, and expects him or her to play some part in the novel.

You may be fascinated by the colourful backgrounds against which your story is set, and some description of them will undoubtedly be attractive and interesting. But don't hold up the story while you go on painting the scene for pages and pages. Keep such descriptions fairly brief, and don't try to put in all the colour and pageantry in one go – intersperse it with action. Remember too that backgrounds are more readily absorbed by the reader if they are seen through the eyes of one of your characters, rather than as a direct statement from you, the author.

This also applies to the mass of fascinating information that you have acquired as a result of research. There is a great temptation to put the lot into your book. If you do, you will probably find that you are not writing a novel at all, but a form of text book. Research is essential, but all successful historical novelists would agree that only a small part of what they learn actually appears in the book – the part that is relevant to your story, and that is important for your reader to know. As with backgrounds: if you want to put your research across to your readers, then do it through the medium of your characters; even then you must be careful that it is always relevant to them and their story – otherwise, the accusation that 'your research is showing' will be justified.

When researching for my first novel, I discovered that much of the city of Genoa had been rebuilt shortly before my hero passed through it on his way to America. As he walked from the station to the docks, I described the new roads and buildings. 'What has this got to do with Mario's story?' my editor asked. 'Your research is showing. Just say that he walked from the station to the docks, and get on with what happened to him there.' I took the advice.

A device which I have found extremely useful, when I have wanted to use the results of my researches into various industries, is to give my main character the need and the opportunity to learn the details of the trade. By showing him in the process of learning, I can also get the information across to my reader, but I always try to make this as interesting as I can, to make the knowledge affect the character concerned, and not to put too much detail in at any one point in the story. Large lumps of research, like long descriptions of the scenery or of your characters' physical appearance, tend to be extremely indigestible, and the reader will probably skip them, which is a waste of all your efforts.

Above all, never lecture your reader. You may have decided that one of the purposes of your novel is to show that Atilla the Hun was not an uncouth marauding barbarian but a man of high culture and great diplomatic skills. Fair enough, if that is what you believe and your research shows you that a case can be made out for your argument. But don't ever put the point over as the author speaking to the reader. You will not only be intruding and forcing yourself and your opinions on the reader, but you will be holding up the story. Allow the information that you wish to present to emerge from the characters themselves and their actions.

Dealing with Time

I have suggested in the chapter on Planning that you need to make a timetable of the events in your novel. How do you get across to your readers the passage of time? There are many ways. You could use a date as a kind of chapter title (descriptive chapter titles are nowadays somewhat out of fashion), or you can use phrases such as 'In the autumn of that year' or 'The following morning' or 'A few days after the festivities' or 'Several years passed before . . .', or you can be specific – 'On Wednesday, 18 April, 1906, shortly after five a.m.' (though you may rightly feel that such precision sounds rather as though the author's research is showing).

You do not always, however, have to indicate the passage of time in so many words. If, for instance, your main character goes to bed at the end of one chapter, the reader will assume that the next chapter begins the following day, unless you make it obvious that a longer period has taken place. Internal evidence can enhance this effect: 'The sun was struggling to find its way through the clouds as Lady Mary walked to the paddock' – that will underline the fact that we are now talking about the next morning. In the same way, if Lady Mary is setting out to travel to London, you don't have to tell your readers exactly how long the journey takes (unless of course the journey itself is important and filled with incident). Leave a blank line, or end the chapter, as she leaves home, and your reader will assume that the next scene, showing her arrival in London, will be a few days later.

Sometimes you may wish to change the time by going back to something which happened earlier than the events you are describing. This device is the 'flashback', and it can be very useful. If your story begins at a moment of crisis, you may well need to tell the reader about what has led up to that point, and one of the best ways of doing so is by flashback, and, naturally, by making a scene of it rather than just narrating what happened.

First of all, you need to indicate to the reader that you are going to go back in time. A simple way of doing this is to begin with your character thinking about the past. Assuming that you are using the past tense for your story, you will now need to go into the pluperfect – that is to say, the form of the verb which uses 'had' as an auxiliary – so you might begin the flashback with a sentence like: 'Lady Mary remembered that some months earlier her father had come home from London. He had come into the Great Hall, stamping his feet angrily.' Now if you continue with a rash of 'hads' they will become very obtrusive, but there is no need to do so. After the first 'had', you can continue by using the simple past tense, so that it reads like this:

Lady Mary remembered that some months earlier her father had come home from London. He came into the Great Hall, stamping his feet angrily. She and her mother ran to meet him apprehensively, knowing that he was in a furious mood.

'The King,' he announced, 'has summoned us all to

London – I myself, you, my lady wife, and you, Mary. This, mark you, is to be considered an honour. Whether we wish it or nay matters naught to him.'

Lady Elizabeth tried to calm him. 'Come, eat! Your tidings will anger you less when your belly is full.'

And so on. When you reach the end of the scene, a simple sentence or two will return your reader to the point in the story where the flashback began: 'Mary laughed to herself as she remembered her father's anger. He had continued to grumble all through the preparations and the journey to London, but now one would think that he had longed all his life to be a courtier.'

Violence and Sex

Although you might think that scenes of violence and graphic sex are essential ingredients in any form of entertainment nowadays, you certainly don't have to include them in your historical novel, any more than you have to lard your dialogue with 'four-letter' words. If they belong in your story, and if you have the desire and the ability to write them effectively, then do so. To include gratuitous violence and blow-by-blow sexual encounters simply because you think it may make your book more saleable is to court disaster. Not only will such passages clearly appear to have been imposed on a story that does not demand them, and not only will they ring false unless you are truly committed to write them and enjoy doing so, but also you will not be aiming at the major market for historical novels, which, apart from bodice-rippers, tends to avoid anything which might be construed as obscene or over-bloodthirsty.

Chapters

How many chapters should your book have? As many as you want, or none at all. Too many very short chapters will give a very jerky effect, while none at all may make the book seem very tedious. Readers expect a certain number of breaks in the narrative, but your chapters do not have to be all of the same length, and whether you have ten or twenty or forty depends on the length and complexity of your novel. You may also wish to divide the book into parts, perhaps jumping a number of years between each part and thus leaving out the duller parts of your characters' lives. If you have no chapters at all, at least there will be breaks indicated by blank lines, which are also often used when the scene, and perhaps the focus of attention, changes within a chapter.

Just as a paragraph is normally concerned with one basic thought, so a chapter is usually concerned with one particular section of your story, and will usually end as that particular episode is completed, or you reach a point in it where there is a 'natural break' (preferably with a cliff-hanger to take the reader on to the next section).

Persevere

The writing of a book demands a great deal of perseverance and self-discipline. Many would-be writers find it a daunting prospect, and stick to their attempts at short-story writing because they cannot face the idea of producing 60,000 words or more. However, if you do want to write a historical novel, don't allow yourself to be put off by the amount of effort involved. Keep at it. Write as regularly as you can. Set yourself a realistic target of the number of words you will produce every week, and do your level best to keep to it.

One of the best bits of advice that practised writers give is to leave off at the end of a day when you know what will come next – even in the middle of a sentence – because then you will find it easier to start the next time you begin work. I find that my detailed synopsis is a great help in this respect, because I always know what is to come next.

You may find that part way through the book, you begin to flag. You feel that your writing is boring and that no one will ever want to read it. Take heart. Most novelists I know confess to similar feelings. Don't give up, but press on to the end. When you come to revise your work (see the chapter on Revision) you may be pleasantly surprised at how readable and un-boring that particular passage is, and if it does sag, you can probably cut or rewrite it until it flows as well as the rest of the story.

The Magic Ingredient

You can take all the good advice in this book, you can listen to and learn from Creative Writing tutors, you can pick the brains of established writers – in short, you can make every effort to study and learn your craft – but there is still one thing you need, and that is the Magic Ingredient.

The Magic Ingredient is something that no book or tutor can teach you. It is not even easy to describe, but it is that little extra something which will make your book special. It is to do with the art of telling a story and with keeping your readers totally involved, so that they love every word.

If you do not have that innate story-telling ability, and if nobody can teach you how to acquire it, what on earth can you do about it? First of all, let me say that you may already have it, without being aware of it, for it is something which comes from the subconscious, and it may well reveal itself when you come to write your book. Even if it doesn't appear at once, don't abandon hope, because it often comes with practice.

If you write your book with total enthusiasm; if you relish every word as you set it down; if the characters and events of your novel become more real to you than the world in which you live; if you find excitement in the development of the story and even surprise yourself with the power with which it grows; *and* if you yet remain in control of it all – then, oh, then, you will be near to finding, or may have already found, the Magic Ingredient.

6

BEGINNINGS AND ENDINGS

Where to Start

The first words of a novel are of vital importance. You need to interest your readers immediately, and one of the best ways of doing this is to plunge immediately into some kind of action. As already explained, I do not necessarily mean physical action, but a scene in which there is tension and conflict. If you begin by describing the background, and especially if you try to tell the reader in narrative form what has happened before the point at which your story really opens, you will probably have a dull beginning.

If you can put questions in your readers' minds right at the beginning you will arouse their interest, and that is another reason for starting off without explanation of what is going on or who the characters are. You want your readers to ask, 'Who is this person?', 'Why is she saying that?', 'Why are they all so frightened?', 'What is this great event they are talking about?', and so on. Of course, you must not confuse your readers with too many such questions, and you must soon begin to make plain who the characters are and what is going on, or at least to give hints as to the answers – if you don't, the readers will quickly get bored – but each question that you do succeed in posing in this way is a hook to make your readers want to go on.

You can begin with a really startling sentence: 'The man plunged the dagger deep into his mother's breast.' That should interest any reader, and provoke questions: 'Who is the man?' 'Why is he apparently murdering his mother?' The one problem with an extremely dramatic opening of this sort is that it will almost certainly be difficult to live up to it – to keep the tension going at the same rate – and there is nothing more guaranteed to disappoint a reader than a wildly startling beginning which is followed by a much lower level of excitement. Most authors will wisely prefer a somewhat quieter approach from which they can build. However, there is nothing to stop you using something which may be less dramatic, but which is equally intriguing.

I always try to introduce my main character in the very first line of the novel, naming him or her, but not at that point giving any physical description or other detailed information. I hope that this will indicate to my readers that this is the person in whom I want them to be interested, with whom I want them to identify. I also hope that the first of the questions that they will ask themselves is 'Who is this person?', especially since I usually give the character's first name only.

The next important thing to do, as has already been suggested, is to present that main character in a scene which comes at a crisis point, or immediately before it, which will affect him or her, and which is the beginning of the whole story, the incident without which none of it might have happened. Again, although it should be dramatic, make sure that it is not more dramatic than the events which are going to follow.

Because you present this crisis point as a scene, rather than in narration, you will be able to use dialogue to answer the questions which you initially raise in your readers' minds, and to put over a certain amount of information. You may at the same time be able to introduce other characters, and to give some indication of where the scene is taking place, though I would suggest that you should do so as economically as possible, for too much information, especially at the beginning of a story, may prove indigestible.

It is also a good idea to give, if you can, some suggestion of what kind of story is to follow, though this is sometimes difficult to do, and is not as important a point as the others which have been mentioned. In any case, your title may have already made it pretty clear.

What is perhaps more essential is to present, as soon as you can, some information from which the reader can deduce the period of the novel. You can do this, of course, by starting off, for instance, with such a sentence as 'It was Christmas Day in the year of Our Lord 1491.' But there are subtler and more effective ways (incidentally, do try to avoid 'the year of Our Lord' – admittedly, it has a sort of archaic ring, but through overuse by modern historical novelists it has become boring).

To see how some of these points can work in practice, here are the opening lines of my novel *The Silk Maker:*

> 'See who it is, then, Richard.'
>
> The knock on the door was repeated, falling threateningly into the dimly lit, silent room. Richard ran to open the door, and sunlight flooded in.
>
> 'Is your mother at home, boy?'
>
> 'Aye, missus.'
>
> 'Call me by my name, boy. You know who I am, surely.'
>
> Richard knew her well. Her fashionable bonnet blocked his view every Sunday in church, and when

the congregation left after the service, sometimes she would glance at his parents in distant acknowledgement of the little bow that his father always gave. She was Mrs Charlotte Harcourt, wife to the owner of the silk mill where Richard's father worked . . . had worked.

'Please enter, ma'am,' Richard's mother called. She was standing now, her knuckles gleaming white as she gripped the back of the hardwood chair.

Mrs Harcourt fastidiously gathered in her skirts so that they should not brush against the doorway. Richard could hear the rustle of her silk plaid-patterned dress, and the many skirts she wore beneath it, as she walked into the room. 'I come to offer you my condolences, Mrs Goodwin.'

'You are very kind, ma'am. Will you not take a chair?'

In the light of the single candle which illuminated the sparsely furnished room, Mrs Harcourt could not be sure that the seat was clean. She gave a little wave of the hand to indicate that she would not sit, and drew her shawl about her shoulders. Her gaze settled on the dozen or so books which stood on the mantelshelf, and she sniffed in disapproval. Books! A family like the Goodwins had no business with books – except, of course, the Bible . . . 'Your husband's death must have been a great shock.'

'I still find it difficult to believe.'

There was a strange tone in his mother's voice, and Richard looked at her, wondering if she were going to weep again; but her eyes, though red-rimmed, were clear. He glanced at his sisters. Mary and Frances were huddled together by the fireplace. He knew somehow that they felt the same uneasiness.

'How old was he? Do you know when he was born?' So few women of Mrs Goodwin's class bothered with such details.

'He was born on the twenty-fourth of March in the year of our Lord eighteen hundred and five.'

Mrs Harcourt looked at her sharply. Was the woman trying to be impertinent? She decided to ignore it. 'Forty-seven is no age. No age at all. Had he complained of feeling unwell?'

'He was in good health and spirits as he left for work that day,' Elizabeth Goodwin replied. 'Then they came and told me that he was dead.'

'A seizure of the heart.'

'So they say.'

'It is unusual in someone so thin. He was very thin, your husband. Undernourished, perhaps.'

'My husband never wanted for food.'

'You cannot deceive me, Mrs Goodwin. Oh, if only people would think before they bring children into the world! You have three, alas – three hungry mouths to feed – and no doubt you and your husband starved for their sake. Such folly! Look at you – you are just skin and bones yourself.'

Richard glanced at his mother again. True, she was thin, but why, he wondered, should Mrs Harcourt say so in such an angry way. She was skinny herself, but whereas his mother's thinness was somehow friendly and comfortable, Mrs Harcourt's was hard and . . . spiky. He decided suddenly that he hated Mrs Harcourt, with her brightly rouged cheeks, and her scent which filled the cottage with its unnatural, pungent smell.

'It is all very well for us women,' she was saying. 'Our constitutions are so made that we can accept privation – but men require adequate nourishment.'

'William was well fed.' Elizabeth's voice was still the same monotone, as though she dared not allow herself to express any emotion. 'It was work that killed him. He gave his life to the mill.'

Mrs Harcourt bridled. 'Mr Harcourt is the most generous, the most considerate of employers.'

'I know that, Mrs Harcourt.'

'I should hope so. Too generous, too considerate. Besides, hard work never killed anyone.'

Richard saw his mother's eyes flash briefly, but she said nothing.

While I am not saying that this extract could not be improved, it does demonstrate much of the advice given above.

The first line is not in any way startling, but Richard, who is named in it, is indeed the central character. In the first few paragraphs I give no information about him, except that there may be a clue to his age in the fact that he runs to open the door, suggesting that he is a child. This suggestion is reinforced as the scene continues. Although there are brief excursions into Mrs Harcourt's thoughts, the scene is described mainly from Richard's viewpoint, which again establishes his importance.

Questions are, I hope, raised in my readers' minds during the first twenty lines or so: 'Who is Richard?' 'Why is the room dimly lit when there is bright sunshine outside?' 'Why has Mrs Harcourt come to call?' As the scene progresses, answers gradually emerge.

The story begins at a moment of crisis in Richard's life. The sudden death of his father, leaving his family penniless (as we discover as the novel continues), radically changes Richard's life. Nothing that follows would have happened had it not been for this event. At the same time, although a death in the family is always a dramatic event (and is often used as the starting point of a novel), it is not as filled with conflict and tension as some of the scenes which will come later in the story.

Although the theme of the book is not clearly stated at this point, at least some hint of it is given – it is in fact, in very simple terms, concerned with Richard's rise to the top of the silk-manufacturing industry and his continuing hatred of the Harcourt family. The title of the book – *The Silk Maker* – together with the references in the scene to the silk mill give a pretty clear indication that the industry will be the background of the story. The contrast between Mrs Harcourt's affluence and the Goodwins' poverty, and the obvious differences in their respective social standings hint to the reader that the theme of the conflict between the two families will be followed through.

Note also that the story begins with a scene, during which a great deal of information is brought before the reader, almost all of it emerging from the dialogue. Three main characters (Richard, Elizabeth and Mrs Harcourt) are introduced, and Mary and Frances are briefly mentioned.

The novel could have started like this: 'Richard Goodwin's father, William, had worked as an overseer at Harcourt's Silk Mill in Brentfield for many years. It was a great shock to his wife Elizabeth, and his other children, Mary and Frances, when in 1852 he died suddenly of a heart attack. The wife of the owner of the mill came, with great condescension, to see the widow.'

If the opening had been like that – narration rather than action – there would have been no questions in my readers' mind (except, perhaps, as to which of the characters named they were supposed to be interested in). Characters would not have been established, and the focus on Richard would not have been as clear. Indeed, it could have been adequate as the opening paragraph of a synopsis, but not as the beginning of a novel.

As for the period of the story, there are many clues in the first few paragraphs, especially in the descriptions of Mrs Harcourt's clothes – her bonnet, the fact that she had to gather in her skirts so that they should not brush against the doorway, the many skirts which she wore beneath her dress, her shawl. Additional indications are the way in which Richard's mother speaks – 'Will you not take a chair?', and her use of 'ma'am' – and indeed both her attitude and that of Mrs Harcourt. The candle is yet another clue. I think (at least, I hope) most readers would realise that we are in the nineteenth century, at the time when wide skirts were fashionable and when the 'gentry' condescended to the 'lower orders'.

Attentive readers will have noticed that, despite suggesting earlier that the words 'in the year of our Lord' are somewhat clumsy, I allowed Elizabeth to use them. She does so, in fact, with some irony, and Mrs Harcourt is right to think that she is perhaps being impertinent.

Finally, there is the setting of the scene. How much information are my readers given? They are told that the room is dimly lit by a single candle, and that is sparsely furnished. The only furniture mentioned is a hardwood chair. There is a fireplace, and books stand on the mantelshelf. It is hardly a full description, yet I think that it is sufficient for readers to picture the room in some detail.

It is an interesting exercise to read the openings of other published historical novels. How have those authors coped with the problems? Have they used the techniques that I have recommended? Have they been more or less successful than I have?

When you begin your own novel, take the greatest of care with the opening paragraphs and the material which immediately follows. Make a scene of it. Ask yourself whether you have begun at the right place – not too far back in your story so that you have not yet arrived at a moment of tension. Is there sufficient impact, and have you raised questions in your readers' minds? Have you focused attention on your principal character? Have you established the period, and perhaps given some indication of what the story is to be about? Have you written economically, and is everything in the opening relevant?

Where to End

It is usually easier to find an effective ending than to begin well.

There are two main pitfalls to avoid. The first is reaching the end too suddenly, so that while your hero and heroine may have finished up happily in each other's arms, you have left all sorts of other loose ends untied, and have to add a hasty round-up, sometimes in the form of an epilogue, to tidy the whole thing up. Plan your last chapter carefully, and tie up the loose ends, saying all that needs to be said about the less important characters before you come to the last pages, so that the final words can be devoted to the true climax of the story.

The second fault demonstrated by many would-be authors is their apparent inability to resist adding at the very end some comment of their own. 'Thus ends the story of Mary Whatshername and Henry VIII.' Cut any such sentence or paragraph. Remember, too, that your readers are intelligent, and can work some things out for themselves. For adults the Cinderella story is over as soon as the glass slipper fits – they don't need to be told that Cinderella and the Prince were married and lived happily ever after.

Your aim should be for your readers to put the book down when they reach the end with a sense of satisfaction and fulfilment, and not feeling that they have been left halfway through the story. You may leave them with some questions in their mind as to what happens next – indeed, you may do so deliberately, with the plan of writing a sequel – but at least for the moment, everything should seem settled, without any hint of major dramas to come in the immediate future.

Your protagonists should have grown, have been changed by the events of your story, and the ambition which has driven your central character, or the goal to which he or she was aiming, must have been achieved or reached. Justice must also be seen to have been done, and your villains should have received their come-uppance. On the other hand, it may not always mean that your hero or heroine has triumphed; if Lady Mary Whatshername is sent home at the end of your novel, defeated by Katherine Howard, justice will be seen to have been done if she has, at least to some extent, brought this fate upon herself.

Most readers prefer, I think, an up-beat ending – what a shame it would be if the slipper did not fit Cinderella and the Prince went away, leaving her to a life of drudgery.

But not all stories can end with your hero and heroine embarking on a life in which there will be henceforward nothing but happiness and success. You may want to finish with the death of your central character (which will not necessarily have too much of a down-beat effect if his or her life was one of fulfilment). The important point is that there should be a feeling of inevitability about the ending, which has been generated by the people in the story. Be careful not to impose a conventional happy ending on your story if it does not really seem credible for your characters. The first draft of my novel, *The Silk Maker,* ended with the hero and heroine, Richard and Sarah, about to marry, but my editor pointed out that Richard would not have accepted the terms for their partnership which Sarah was suggesting. My editor was right, and I therefore contrived an alternative ending, though still with a strong element of the up-beat. I believe it disappointed some readers, but it was certainly much more true to the characters I had established.

Sometimes the ending of a historical novel is dictated by the facts of history. If we take yet again the story of Lady Mary Whatshername, it is obvious that she is going to be defeated at the end when Henry marries Katherine Howard. So we shall have something of a down-beat ending. If we leave Mary feeling bitter and sorry for herself, it will be very unsatisfactory; if, on the other hand, we have allowed her to grow and develop during the course of the novel, we could perhaps see her in the final pages thinking back without regrets on the relationship she had had with the King, and, since she knows how inconstant both he and Katherine can be, wondering how long the marriage will last. Being older and wiser than at the beginning of the story, she might even generously hope that Katherine would make Henry happy, and that their union would be a lasting one (and that, of course, would be a final touch of dramatic irony, for the reader will be aware that Katherine ended up with her head on the block – some nineteen months, in fact, after she became Queen).

7

DIALOGUE

Dialogue in General

Dialogue is an essential part of the novel. Beginners often ask how much of it should there be. Well, there have been a few successful novels which have dispensed with it almost entirely, and others, like those of Ivy Compton-Burnett which consist virtually of nothing but dialogue. For their romantic novels Mills & Boon, for instance, ask that fifty per cent of the story should consist of dialogue, but generally speaking there are no rules about how much of it to include.

However, several justifications can be given for using a fair amount of dialogue. We have already seen that it is vitally important to make a scene of the high spots in your story, and if the action is to be presented in front of the reader's eyes, it will undoubtedly include dialogue. Dialogue is one of the most satisfactory ways of giving the reader essential information, of conveying conflict and of advancing your story. Finally, dialogue is always, or should be, revealing of character, and should help you to build up a convincing and interesting picture of the people in your novel.

Since speech is the most common form of human communication, it should be easy to write dialogue, but this is not in fact the case. You must aim at producing your characters' words in a way which will sound natural, which will be in keeping with their characters, and which will have colour, sparkle, rhythm and flow. This is a difficult thing to bring off successfully, especially in the historical novel, in which you may be trying to convey modes of speech which differ from those we use in ordinary twentieth-century conversation. Some specific points on achieving a period flavour in your dialogue will be found below.

One of the main problems in fictional dialogue is that, while it must *sound* natural, in fact it will be completely artificial. In normal conversation, we hesitate, repeat ourselves, fail to finish sentences, and meander all over the place. If we reproduce faithfully the way we normally speak, the result would be extremely tedious, if not unreadable. Moreover, we engage continually in fairly meaningless waffle, partly out of the conventions of polite social intercourse, and partly out of a sheer need to fill silences with chatter. Turn on a voice recorder of whatever description you possess, and you might get something like this:

> 'Good morning.'
> 'Good morning.'
> 'Did you – did you sleep well?'
> 'Yes, thanks. Looks like a nice day.'
> 'What?'
> 'I said it looks like a nice day.'
> 'Oh. Yes. I know what I – er – what I meant to ... Oh, dammit now it's gone right out of my ... Oh, I know – you remember where we'd got to last night about —'
> 'I say! Look at that woman over there.'
> 'Which one? Oh, I see. Yes, she's certainly —'

'Sorry. What were you saying?'

And so on. That kind of dialogue must be cut ruthlessly. Readers do not want to read social chit-chat, and will happily take it for granted that your characters would probably indulge in it without your having to set it down for them. You must edit your dialogue so that it is economical and contains nothing that is not essential either to establish character or to move the story forward. Hesitations and interruptions can occasionally be used to good effect, but their too frequent use will result in the dialogue sounding jerky and losing a sense of flow and rhythm.

Effective dialogue is in some respects like a good rally at tennis or table tennis. Someone starts the rally by serving, and the ball flashes backwards and forwards over the net according to how the player responds to the placing of the ball by the opponent and the efforts made to finish the rally. In the same way, a dialogue between two characters begins with one saying something and the other responding, and as it continues each response is dictated by what has been said. Your characters must listen to each other. If you record a conversation on tape, cut out the chit-chat, and then see how the dialogue develops. There may be points when one person does not listen to the other (and that device can sometimes be used effectively), but for the most part each speech will spring from the one preceding it. Sometimes, something which is said, even a single word, will totally change the direction of the conversation, and that too is the kind of thing which you can use to make your dialogue sound natural (but don't allow it to happen unless you mean it to do so).

It is very important to make sure that your characters are consistent in the way they speak. If you have worked on the characterisations so that you really know your people thoroughly, you should be able to hear them speak, and if you know the emotions that they are to express, or the news they are to convey, or how they would react to whatever the person to whom they are talking is saying, then you should have little difficulty in giving them their own particular voice.

Liveliness and rhythm and flow come from dialogue which is in character, which advances the story, which is to the point, and which has variety in the length of the spoken sentences. It will be enhanced sometimes by wit or humour, and by changes of mood. Above all, it will be economical. In real life we rarely have enough time to think about what we are saying, with the result that we often fail to say what we mean, and have to go back to explain ourselves; in the novel, on the other hand, although every line of dialogue must sound natural, it will be as though your characters have thought out their words in advance, so that they do mean exactly what they say, at least when they are telling the truth. If they are lying, the words will still have been carefully worked out, just as they will if the character is apparently speaking thoughtlessly, and the precision of the dialogue may not on occasion prevent other characters from misunderstanding what they hear.

One special problem in making the dialogue sound natural comes when you are dealing with a crowd scene It is all too easy, especially sometimes for the historical novelist, to write something like: 'We will have none of her and her fancy ways, her powder and paint!' shouted the crowd. 'To the guillotine with her without delay!' That comes into the category of what *The New Yorker* might have called 'Shouts we doubt were ever shouted'. Give lines of dialogue to individual members of the crowd, and keep them short and pithy, and as natural as possible. A better answer might be simply to tell the reader in narration that the crowd were calling for this lady's execution, especially as there would probably be plenty of action going on to keep the scene alive.

Making the Meaning Clear

When we speak in real life we use many devices in addition to the words to make sure that our listeners understand us – the expression in our voices and on our faces, emphases, gestures, differing paces, pauses, and so on, added to which, if the listener is in any doubt, he or she has the opportunity of asking us to go back over what we have said, or to provide further explanations. In the novel you have only the printed words to convey the meaning. To some extent we can make it easier for the reader with punctuation, including underlining (to indicate italics) for emphasis, and by using adverbs or adverbial phrases to describe the tone of voice.

You can also show pauses by a narrative interruption: 'Said she that?' Henry said softly, a dangerous tone in his voice. He walked over to the window. 'Why should I believe *your* word against that of others?' He turned to face him, frowning. 'Send her to me!' he commanded. But try, as hard as you can, to make the words of the dialogue do all the work, so that your readers will automatically understand and will be able to add for themselves the subtleties of expression and mood.

Do, by the way, try to avoid the use of too many adverbs to amplify the dialogue. At the end of the example just given, we could add the word 'peremptorily'. But it's not necessary, because the command was obviously given in a peremptory way. Note too that, for the same reason, we could also dispense with 'he commanded'.

Attributions

The term 'attribution' is used to describe the words which tell us who is speaking – 'he said', 'I replied', 'Lady Mary said'. Be assured that, while in your writing you should avoid obtrusive repetitions (unless you are using them for a special effect), you can go on using 'said' until the cows come home, and your readers will not notice the lack of variety. You can legitimately also use 'asked', 'replied', 'answered', and an occasional 'shouted' or 'laughed', but please don't feel any necessity to avoid 'said' by the substitution of words like 'gritted' or 'gloomed' or 'worried' or similar absurdities. And I always think it preferable to eschew also such attributions as 'came the reply' or, worse, 'came the swift rejoinder'.

Of course, you do not need to attribute every speech. If two people are talking and you follow the suggestions for paragraphing described below, the reader will be able to tell which person is speaking, especially if the dialogue is very much in character, provided that the dialogue does not go on for too long without an attribution. You can identify the speaker too by including in his or her dialogue the name of the person spoken to, or if you interrupt his or her speech with a brief piece of narrative, by naming him or her when you do so. For example:

> *'Said she that?' Henry walked over to the window.*
> *'Send her to me, Cromwell.'*
> *'Yes, your Majesty.'*

That duologue could continue for several lines without any formal attributions, but equally without any doubt in the reader's mind as to which of the characters was speaking.

Paragraphing the Dialogue

It is best to break up a section of dialogue by giving a new paragraph to each person who speaks. If you interrupt one character's speech by a line of narrative describing that person's actions, that line and all that he or she says before or after the interruption can be included in one paragraph (see Henry's dialogue in the example above). To run several speeches by different people into one paragraph, or to add a narrative line about one of your characters on to a speech by a different character will confuse the reader.

Open quotation marks at the beginning of each speech, and close them when the person stops talking. If you give a character a very long speech (which, incidentally, it will probably be as well to break up by narrative interruptions), you may want to divide it into paragraphs; if so, do not close the quotation marks at the end of the first paragraph, but re-open them at the beginning of the next paragraph; repeat this for subsequent paragraphs, until the end of the speech, and only then close the quotes.

Thoughts

Writers are often bothered by the question of how to show a character's thoughts. One of the great advantages that the novelist has is the ability to get inside a character's mind and to show the reader what that person is thinking, especially if the thought is in contrast with what he or she is saying or doing. Should you put the thoughts in inverted commas, as though it were a line of dialogue? Should you perhaps put them in italics? Either is possible, though I think the former idea can be confusing, and the latter looks rather clumsy. I prefer in my novels always to put thoughts into a reported form – 'He thought that she believed him, but could not be sure.'

Dialogue in the Historical Novel

The English language is constantly changing. We do not speak the same way today as we did even as little as twenty years ago. New words, new phrases, new rhythms of speech, and new meanings for old words constantly appear – an obvious case in point is the fact that we can only very rarely use that charming word 'gay' to mean 'merry, bright and cheerful' (only, in fact, if the context is such that no hint of homosexuality will be put into the reader's mind).

It is in the dialogue that the difference between present-day English and that of the past will most clearly be seen. The characters in any historical novel will not speak as we would today. On the other hand, if the writer renders their speech with complete accuracy, the result may seem very mannered and even incomprehensible, and the farther back in time you go, the worse the problem becomes.

Some sort of compromise is needed – a language which suggests a period flavour, and which avoids anachronisms. You will not achieve the period flavour by the insertion of words and phrases such as 'by halidom!' or 'stap me vitals'. This kind of usage is sometimes known as 'God-wottery', an allusion to the poem which begins 'A garden is a lovesome thing, God wot!' (not, as you might think, the work of a fifteenth-century poet, but written by one T. E. Brown, who died in 1897). God-wottery can become very obtrusive, and almost always has a false sound to it. Equally, try not to lard your work with obscure words which may be historically accurate but which will not mean much to modern readers; if they are essential, then, as neatly as you can, explain them. The avoidance of linguistic anachronisms is just as important – nothing can destroy a sense of period more rapidly than a word or phrase which sounds as though it belongs to the present day. Some American writers are unfortunately particularly prone to this fault.

So how do you achieve this period flavour? If your setting is earlier than the late-sixteenth century, there are few contemporary models which you can acceptably use, but from that time on there is a vast legacy of literature which can help you, from Shakespeare on through the King James Bible, the Restoration dramatists, Defoe, Fielding, Sheridan, Scott, Austen, the Brontes, Dickens, and of course many more. Note that the classic poets are not included in the list – in general, you will find the dramatists and novelists more helpful. At the same, use caution. If you were, for instance, to follow too closely the idiosyncratic exchange of v's for w's and vice versa which Dickens gives to his Cockney characters ('Werry fine veather'), the result would probably not work as well for you as it did for old Charles. But you will certainly be able to use "Tis' or "Twas' in place of 'It is' or 'It was', or 'I vow' in place of 'I believe' if that sort of language is appropriate to your period. But above all try to capture the rhythm of period speech, which will be more effective and less obtrusive, if you are successful, than the introduction of too many mannerisms of the age concerned.

There are some devices in forms of address that will help to give the period feel in your dialogue. For instance, up to the end of the nineteenth century, and even beyond, 'sir' and 'madam' were widely used as a formal form of address, even among friends, while from the seventeenth to the nineteenth centuries husbands and wives often called each other 'Mr —' or 'Mrs —' ('Mr Bennet' or 'Mrs Bennet' in *Pride and Prejudice,* for example), first names being used principally for children and servants. There are many other examples that could be quoted – if you go back a bit farther in time, you find the use of

'Mistress' instead of 'Mrs', 'Mother' for almost any old woman of the poorer classes, 'sire' instead of 'your Majesty', and a whole string of other terms of address – 'lady', 'wench', 'master', 'fellow', 'bully', 'sirrah', 'varlet', and so on. But do be careful – words like 'bully' and 'varlet', not to mention 'scurvy knave', can easily verge on God-wottery.

For a novel set earlier than the seventeenth century, you may be tempted to use 'thou', 'thee' and 'thy' for the second person singular, but you need to take great care. The problem is that those forms demand that you should also use the appropriate form of verb, and you may find yourself writing such a line of dialogue as 'Thou knowest who I am. I know that thou despisest me. Understandest thou that I in turn hate thee, thee and all thy clan? Thou art a mean cur!' The result is undeniably clumsy, and will rapidly lose your reader's attention. To make matters worse, you should probably be logical and use the archaic inflexion for third person singular verbs – 'he saith', 'she cometh', and so on. It is probably better to avoid these archaic forms, and stick to 'you'.

In general, the best advice is to use simple English, but a slightly more formal mode of speech than we would use in conversation today will probably be appropriate ('You cannot mean it', for example, rather than 'You can't mean it') – though some contractions can certainly be used, including 'ain't', which is nowadays considered to be bad English, but which in past times was often widely used by the educated classes. Provided that you don't overdo it, the elimination in questions of the verb 'do', which nowadays we use so often, and a switch in positions of the subject and the verb will also suggest a period atmosphere ('How came you here?' rather than 'How did you get here?', 'Know you not?' rather than 'Do you not know?'). It is not easy to get this right, and if you are following the advice to be a little more formal than in modern speech you must beware of making all your characters sound too pompous as a result.

Period slang and phrases can be added, and they will give extra life, but do make sure that they are in period. A good dictionary can be of great assistance, because it will usually tell you when a certain word first came into use. In one of my novels, set in Victorian times, I had one character referring to another as 'a git' (the slang word meaning 'a worthless person'); it sounded to me like one of those words which has been around for centuries – I could imagine a character in some Elizabethan play saying, 'Thou knave, thou whoreson git!' – but the Dictionary told me the word was coined in 1941, and I had to change it. For slang, in particular, a Dictionary of Historical Slang is very useful, particularly regarding the dates when the words concerned were used.

It is essential, of course, that any slang or period words that you use should be readily comprehensible to the average reader. If, for instance, your story is set in the late-thirteenth century and you have a lady complimenting another by saying, 'I like well your barbette' or commenting on the new fashion among men of winding their lirapipes around their heads, you will be making it clear that you have done your research well, but your reader may not have the least idea of what you are talking about, unless you explain that a barbette was a linen band which women wound round their heads and under their chins, while a lirapipe was a long tail-like appendage on men's hats.

Four-letter words

Most of the so-called four-letter words in current use have a long history, and were undoubtedly used by our forebears. However, the fact that they have become printable only in the past few decades gives them, when they appear in a book, a feeling of modernity, and you will probably be well-advised to avoid using them. There are plenty of swear-words and terms of abuse which will sound almost as strong, and which will more easily maintain the period atmosphere. If you particularly want to use an expletive for its shock effect, remember that it loses that quality if it is repeated too often – one four-letter word in a novel will be startling and effective, while a hundred will simply become tiresome. In any case, the average reader of historical novels, I venture to suggest, would prefer them not to be awash with obscenities.

Dialects

While most of your dialogue will probably be written in standard English, or a period form of it – in other words, the speech of educated persons of the time – you may also have to write dialogue for the 'lower orders'. If they live in the country, you may use some kind of Mummerset, or perhaps an accent, and if they come, say, from London or the Deep South, you will probably want to use something which suggests this. Do so by all means, but do it in moderation. It can be very tiresome to read a long passage in which every *h* is dropped and every *th* at the end of a word turned into a *v* or an *f*. You can often suggest an accent, simply by telling your reader that the character concerned speaks in a certain way, without trying to reproduce the speech phonetically. And you can try to indicate a dialect too by using the cadences and the idioms of the region – 'wee' and 'mon' and 'och' suggest a Scot, and 'begorrah' an Irishman. However, try to avoid relying entirely on such hackneyed words as those.

Anachronisms

Naturally you want everything in your dialogue to be in period, or at least to sound suitable for the age in which your story is set. Anything which smacks of the twentieth century will be out of place, but this is not only a matter of words and phrases. If you were to write, 'I think your barbette looks smashing', it would be pretty obvious to you, I hope, that 'smashing' is not likely to have been the word that a thirteenth-century character would have used, but it is not only that word which jars – the whole sentence sounds completely modern, apart from the barbette itself. The problem of anachronisms is in fact much wider than that of a single word or short phrase. Read through all your dialogue to check whether any of it has a modern ring, even if there are no words or phrases which belong specifically to the present day, and alter it appropriately if you possibly can.

8

A SENSE OF PERIOD

The Language of the Historical Novel

How do you put a sense of period into your novel? Research, and the reading of authors contemporary at the time will probably give you most of the pointers you need. But do you need to write in a special way?

The problems of writing dialogue with a period flavour have already been dealt with in the chapter on Dialogue. What about the rest of your text? Much of what has been said about dialogue is relevant here – you need to avoid over-flowery period language and obscure words which will baffle your reader. God-wottery is no more acceptable in the text than in the dialogue – you may have discovered that beer, nowadays still thought of as primarily a drink for men, was for centuries drunk freely by both sexes, but you don't have to make your characters 'quaff' their ale. In other words, don't try to write in a self-consciously historical style.

You do not even need to extend to the rest of the text the suggestion that I made in the chapter on Dialogue of using a slightly more formal language than is common in present-day speech. Good plain modern English is what is needed, provided that you do not include words which are recent innovations, or which have acquired new meanings, or which seem otherwise out of place in your chosen period. Don't, by the way, use archaic spellings. Jane Austen may render it as 'chuse', but you should spell it 'choose', and indeed, stick closely to standard contemporary spelling throughout.

English offers us a choice between words with Anglo-Saxon roots and those that have come to us via Latin and Norman French, and you may feel tempted to use a great many Romance-language words on the grounds that they sound somehow more old-fashioned. Most of them are longer and more likely to sound pompous than the Anglo-Saxon equivalents ('domicile', for instance, as opposed to 'home')! Naturally, there will be occasions when, for the sake of variety, you will use them, but if in doubt, always choose the Anglo-Saxon version, whether for your dialogue or for the narrative.

This last piece of advice applies particularly to your action scenes, and the more rapid and exciting the scene, the more you need to avoid long polysyllabic words, choosing instead short, direct and possibly harsh words, which will reflect the speed of the action and its nature. Almost certainly, your sentences will be shorter too. You will probably find that this comes naturally – if the scene is exciting and fast-moving in your mind, you will set it down on paper so that it reads in the same way.

In short, as with any other prose that you write, you should aim at a style which is economical and has a sense of rhythm and colour, but which is, above all, unobtrusive.

Period Details

You will achieve a period flavour in your novel by the presentation of authentic background details far more than by using a special form of language. A brief description of a character's costume, for instance, will often give a clear indication of the period, and many other markers can also be used, such as food and drink, heating, lighting, forms of transport, housing, and so on – in short, the way people lived, and died, not forgetting social attitudes. It pays to get these details right, and if some of them are particularly strange or colourful, your readers will enjoy hearing about them.

You should have absorbed so much of the background of your chosen century during your research that you will find it easy to avoid mistakes. However, I think it is worth listing some specific points which will repay care. The selection may seem arbitrary, but in my experience it is on matters such as these that would-be historical novelists often trip up.

Attitudes towards Women

I have already written at some length in the chapter on Characterisation about the fact that the position of women in society has been one of subservience until comparatively recently. If you choose as your heroine a spirited, strong-willed lady, with great independence of mind, remember that to her other difficulties may well be added the displeasure of the society in which she moves. Look at Elizabeth Bennet in *Pride and Prejudice* – she is regarded by many of the other characters in the novel as wilful and impertinent, but even Mr Bennet is becomes concerned about her refusal to conform, and this in an age which was probably more tolerant than any period other than our own.

Of course, these attitudes have one great advantage for the historical novelist, because they form a barrier which your determined heroine will have to overcome, and her struggle against convention and the reactions of others towards her can form an important part, if not the whole, of the main plot.

If you want to be realistic, it is probably wise not to let your heroine get married until the end of your story, not merely because it will give you a satisfactorily romantic conclusion, but because, once she had a husband, a woman could spend much of the rest of her life in a state of pregnancy, and had scarcely weaned one baby before the next was born.

Adultery was undoubtedly as popular a pastime in bygone ages as it is now, but the idea of living together before marriage was virtually unknown, at least among the middle and upper classes, although life-time pairings among the lower orders might well happen without the benefit of a church ceremony. Illegitimate children were born, too, of course, and it is worth remembering that bastards were widely acknowledged by their fathers, and only in Victorian times did the stigma which was attached to them, and also to their mothers, become of major significance.

Class Distinctions

Class distinctions were usually extremely strongly marked, and only in bizarre circumstances would the gentry have any relationship with those of the lower orders, other than that of masters and servants, or landowners and tenants, or employers and workers.

The relationship between the rich and the poor was particularly different too in the fact that on the whole people accepted their station in life – you curtseyed when the Squire went by, accepted with gratitude the patronising gifts that his lady might condescend to bring you, and never queried the fact that you were their inferior.

Remember that, while the gentry could engage in acts of charity, these class differences could over-ride any feelings of pity or concern for others. In my novel, *Mario's Vineyard,* I had planned that my hero would meet the heiress Emily King because he fainted on the sidewalk just outside the mansion in San Francisco where she lived; at that moment she was to be emerging in a horse-drawn trap, and seeing Mario lying on the pavement, she was to stop and have him taken into the house to be cared for. When I came to write it, I realised that in 1880, when this was taking place, Emily King would certainly not have stopped at the sight of an ill-dressed person of the lower classes lying on the pavement, whether he were ill, dying, or merely drunk; she would have averted her eyes, and driven on. So I had to contrive another way for them to meet – a way which, incidentally, turned out not only to be more credible, but also to help in developing the situation which was to follow.

Working Conditions

While the aristocracy and the wealthy middle classes – the idle rich – wondered how to fill their leisure time and took lengthy holidays (although they were not referred to as such), extremely long hours for workers were the norm until the twentieth century, and holidays for more than a day at a time were largely unknown. However, until the Industrial Revolution, the working man could at least enjoy himself not only on Sundays (after the almost obligatory visit to church) but also on Holy Days, which included many saints' days. The medieval fairs, which provided one of the main high-spots of the year, were usually first established on various saints' days, and for centuries continued to provide not only a market but also entertainment. In medieval times, although no doubt servants still had to work, the Twelve Days of Christmas provided a kind of national holiday, in which even the poor had some opportunity of joining.

By the nineteenth century, however, the only day in the year, apart from Sundays, when the majority of factories in England closed was Christmas Day. An important point to realise is that employers did not see anything wrong in their ruthless exploitation of their workers, and no one, apart from a few eccentrically minded philanthropists, considered it extraordinary that children of eight or nine could be sent to work in a factory, or that working people should be short of food and clothing. Many employers looked upon themselves as benevolent and did everything that they considered necessary to care for their employees. But attitudes were different – God had placed the bosses in their station in life, and the workers in theirs, and that was the way it was. As Mrs Alexander happily wrote in her hymn for children:

> The rich man in his castle, The poor man at his gate.
> God made them high or lowly, And order'd their estate.

Illness and Death

Turn back the clock, even a comparatively short number of years, and you will find that death resulting from an illness which today we should regard as no more than a minor inconvenience was commonplace in days gone by. Tuberculosis, for instance, was widespread and almost always fatal until the discovery of the sulfa drugs. Mankind was plagued with many diseases which are now virtually unknown or in most cases easily cured – smallpox, diptheria, tetanus, etc, and even appendicitis.

Life expectancy was short, and this is not surprising, since medicine was primitive, diagnosis more likely to be wrong than right, most modern drugs unknown, and the 'cures' often more debilitating than the disease. The use of anaesthetics was unknown in surgery 150 years ago, and antiseptics were not used until the end of the nineteenth century. As for personal cleanliness, even well into the twentieth century the idea of a daily bath would have been considered eccentric outside the leisured classes (and earlier would have been thought a thoroughly dangerous habit). Until quite recent times, large numbers of the population were born in dirt and lived their lives in surroundings of filth. Water came untreated from springs, containing all manner of dangerous impurities. The stench and squalor of the cities were almost unbelievable – we may complain nowadays of litter-louts, but at least we no longer empty chamber pots into the streets – and in the conditions which prevailed, it was hardly surprising that disease flourished, and death was likely to come sooner rather than later. Indeed, it is a cause for wonder that some men and women of bygone ages managed to survive into old age.

Yet another hazard was childbirth, in which many women died, and infant mortality was horrifyingly high by modern standards. We tend to think of the Victorian era as the period of large families, but in fact women of earlier times often had just as many children, but even more of their offspring died at birth or in childhood.

Unless you want to take a romantic, sanitised view of the past, disease and early death, noisome smells and dirt can play an important part in establishing the background of the historical novel.

Communications

In an age when telephones, radio and television did not exist, news took a very long time to travel far beyond its source. Before the days of the railways and steam ships, communications took even longer. New laws and official announcements could be spread through the country by mounted messengers, and posters would often be put up.

Since, however, a huge proportion of the population could not read or write, communication had to be by word of mouth (promulgated, perhaps, by the local parson or the Town Crier), which meant that many of the common people could easily be ignorant of most of what was going on outside their own small communities, or could hear the information in an inaccurate form.

Travel, too, was very slow, mostly extremely uncomfortable, and indeed hazardous. The macadamising of streets in towns began in the early 1800s, prior to which cobbles were used, but most roads were unmade and often impassable in bad weather. Although an intrepid messenger could clatter down the Great North Road, using relays of horses, it would still take him days rather than hours to travel from Edinburgh to London. If your characters move from one place to another, you have to allow time for them to do so.

Remember, too, that while travel was something which moneyed people could indulge in, lesser mortals would probably spend their entire lives in their own villages, never venturing farther than a nearby town, unless perhaps they were conscripted into an army to go and fight on the Continent (only reachable swiftly by ship when the winds were right) or in the Crusades. Ordinary people did not see any necessity to travel (apart from vagrants, including actors, who were usually hounded and punished for their lack of a fixed abode, and others such as peddlers and messengers). Paul Hyland, in his book *Wight* records the case, which is within living memory, of a man who lived near Newport in the Isle of Wight, and had never seen the sea until he reached a very advanced old age, and Newport is a matter of no more than five miles away from the Solent.

Although major historical events may well have an effect on your story, for many people in olden times the world was a very small place consisting only of their own small community. As a result, by the way, inbreeding was common, which is perhaps why the village idiot was always to be found.

Education

Until the late nineteenth century, a very large proportion of the population could neither read nor write, and even today many children manage somehow to slip through the net and grow to adulthood without these skills. For the well-to-do middle classes, schools and universities, often closely associated with the Church, had been in existence many centuries earlier. Private tuition was often given. This was mainly restricted to boys, but among the aristocracy, despite the subservient role which they were later expected to take, girls too would receive a surprisingly wide education.

Religion

The power of the Church was enormous in medieval times. It was the main educating influence, it was wealthy, it had power of life and death over the whole of Christendom, including the monarchs who were otherwise supreme, and it persecuted relentlessly anyone who rebelled against its authority. The Disestablishment of the Church and the Dissolution of the Monasteries under Henry VIII may have removed much of the Church's wealth and power in England, but it did nothing to stop religious intolerance and persecution. Although the influence of the Church was lessened in the centuries that followed, its influence continued to be strong, and it is perhaps significant to note that in the phrase 'the parson and the squire', the two persons of importance in villages right up to World War II, it is the parson who always comes first. The Victorian era, incidentally, has come to be regarded as a period when church-going was universal, but in fact much of the population at that time was seen in the church only for weddings and funerals.

Particularly in the middle ages, but also in far more recent times, superstitious beliefs were widely held, many of them based on traditions of the Old Religion, which predated Christianity. Almost everyone believed in witchcraft, and an old woman who lived by herself, especially if she had any eccentricities or skill in herbal remedies, was likely to be denounced sooner or later as a witch, and subjected to cruel tests which almost invariably 'proved' her guilt. There was also a widespread acceptance of the supernatural, and it is an interesting fact that most of the ghosts which are still said to be encountered in various country houses are usually of persons who died several centuries ago, and who have been haunting the scenes of their death ever since.

Crime and Punishment

For many centuries human life was cheap. Vast numbers of people died before they were thirty, but not all from disease. Overwork, particularly by those committed to slavery, was a factor. Religious persecution resulted in the death of countless thousands, kings ruled in constant anxiety of rebellion and therefore polished off any potential traitor as soon as possible, and many crimes were punishable by death, from murder down to the stealing of a loaf of bread. No king's conscience appears ever to have been troubled by the number of his loyal courtiers he sent to the block or to the stake, no judge to have found any pity for a starving peasant who had pinched a handful of food. In any case, trials were often as much a travesty of justice as those in totalitarian countries today.

Death was, of course, not the only penalty paid by criminals, and many historical novelists will not wish to neglect the 'picturesque' qualities of such punishments for really minor crimes as the stocks, the pillory, branding and maiming.

Heating and Lighting

Although the Romans had a form of central heating, for much of history the heating of houses was of a nature which today we should consider intolerable. Wood was for the most part the only available fuel – don't be misled by references to coal in the seventeenth century or earlier, which in fact meant charcoal. Medieval colliers were charcoal-burners rather than coal-miners. Winters must have seemed very cold indeed (even with thick, warm clothing), and when you also remember that windows were often no more than open holes, perhaps covered by shutters, the hardiness of people in the Middle Ages is surprising. Except in the larger churches and in palaces, by the way, glass windows were not common until the sixteenth century, and even then would have been an unattainable luxury for the poor.

Gas lighting was not in general use until the second half of the nineteenth century, and electric lighting came considerably later. Until then, candles and oil lamps were the only means of providing artificial light. Until halfway through the eighteenth century, oil lamps consisted of shallow dishes in which the wick gave off rather more smoke than light. The rush lights of medieval times were simply rushes which were burned.

Money

It is comparatively easy to find out the cost of anything that your characters have to pay for in whatever period your novel is set. However, do remember inflation is not a modern problem – it has been with us for many centuries, and is certain to have affected the people in your story, especially if they were poor.

9

REVISION

When teaching Creative Writing, I frequently say that one of the great differences between the amateur writer and the professional is that the former doesn't revise, and the latter does. And the professional doesn't revise just once, but goes over his or her work again and again to get it as perfect as possible. There is a danger in this, which is that you may become so hooked on revision that you never finish the job and get to the stage of submitting it to a publisher, so you have to draw a line at some point and decide that you have finished. But do understand that only a genius gets work right the first time.

If you doubt this last remark, look at the original manuscripts of some of the greatest poets. You will see that they are full of deletions and insertions and re-writings. You may argue that Charles Dickens did not do much in the way of revision, but you have to remember that Dickens *was* a genius, and that he wrote almost all of his work at great speed, keeping to a demanding deadline and with the obligation to produce a set number of words for each instalment of his novels. Besides, I am sure he went over what he had written at least once.

One of the problems in revision is that it is not always easy to be self-critical. You know your work so well, you have laboured over it so long, that it is far from easy to see its faults. For this reason, I always recommend that you should put your first draft away for as long as you can bear, so that when you eventually come back to it, you can read it with comparatively fresh eyes. I have to admit that I do not always follow this advice myself, but this is because my novels have all been fairly long. Since I begin the first draft at the beginning and work all the way through without going back over what I have written, when I come to the end I have more or less forgotten the details of the early chapters, which were written many weeks previously (and indeed am often surprised by what I find).

I usually revise my own work four times. The first time through my main aim is to look at the shape of the story, to see that the narrative has sufficient drive, and that I have achieved in broad terms the effect at which I was aiming. I also look to see how economically I have told my story, and in doing so, usually find quite a lot of unnecessary verbiage. Like most writers, I tend often to over-write when producing the first draft, and it is quite likely that during that first revision I will take out up to twenty per cent of what I have written. At the same time I shall be looking for places where I have under-written – scenes which need building up, instances when I have taken for granted information that I have not given my readers and which they cannot be expected to work out for themselves, and so on. So there is often quite a lot of re-writing to do.

If that is a broad revision, the second is much more a matter of detail, and as I examine the text, I am searching for inconsistencies, awkward phraseology, any lack of rhythm in the prose (including a number of consecutive sentences of the same length and basic formation), and a number of other minor points which I will come to later in this chapter.

The third revision is one of the most important. I read the whole book aloud to myself. The point of doing this is that the ear is often a much better editor than the eye, and you can sometimes hear things which are wrong that you will have skipped over when reading by sight alone. I pay especial attention to the dialogue, making sure that it sounds natural and in character. An even better way of doing this is to get someone else to read your work aloud to you. Because such a person does not know what was in your mind as you wrote, his or her reading can show up not only minor infelicities, but places where your words can be read in a way which you did not intend, altering the meaning or at least the emphasis, and you will need to re-write such passages so that your eventual readers will get the right impression.

These three revisions each take several days, because I work carefully without hurrying and there is usually a considerable amount of re-writing to do. A single chapter may take hours of work before it is right. For the fourth revision I choose a day when I am not going to be disturbed, and then read through the whole book, which should now be in a fairly polished state, from beginning to end in one sitting. By doing this I can keep the whole book in my mind, which has not been so easy when I have been working on it page by page, and the object in this case is to see that all the mechanics of the story work reasonably well, that I have not left loose ends untied, that I have not repeated myself, and so on. During this revision, I do not stop to make any necessary alterations, but simply note them so that I can go back afterwards to put right whatever it may be.

You may prefer some other method of revision. Perhaps you are one of those writers who is happier revising and polishing while actually writing the first draft. If you have a word processor you may well like to work in this way, since it is so easy to change what you have written. Indeed, one of the great blessings of the word processor is that it has taken a lot of the drudgery out of revision. But if you do revise as you go along, you will still need to check through the whole work when it is complete, and you will probably have to do so more than once. Whatever you do, don't shirk the work involved. The more trouble you take, the better chance of publication you will have.

General Points to Look for as you Revise

Firstly, as your read through your work, look for the shape, and make sure that your high spots come in the right places, that they are well presented, that the book rises to its final climax, and that there are no sections which sag. Have you used action rather than narration at all the high spots? Make sure that the sub-plots are interwoven into the main story, and that everything hangs together in a credible way. Are all the characters alive and well differentiated, and is the central character not only fully realised, but sympathetic, so that the reader will identify with him or her? Check the focus of attention, ensuring that you have at no point left your readers uncertain about which characters they are meant to be interested in, or from whose viewpoint the story is being told. Have you managed to convey the atmosphere of the period, and included any historical events which would have affected your characters?

In short, you should ask yourself what the weaknesses of the novel are. Answer as honestly as you can, and then try to improve your work in those respects.

Cutting

Cut ruthlessly.

Every single word in your novel should be there for a purpose – get rid of any that don't fall within that category. This may be much more than a matter of striking out unnecessary adjectives and adverbs (but please do so) – it may involve excising whole scenes, or even chapters if nothing of any consequence happens in them and the chapters on either side could stand on their own with, perhaps, a single linking sentence. Cut anything which is sheer stodge.

Cut explanations which your reader doesn't need. Never ever explain – show, don't tell – and don't underestimate your readers' intelligence by thinking that they can't work things out for themselves.

Cut repetitions – not only the same word used twice or more in the space of a few lines, so that it becomes obtrusive, but cases in which you repeat a fact or a description or whatever it may be. In one of my novels I realised in time to amend it that two of my female characters made virtually identical defences of their refusal to accept the traditional Victorian view of a woman's place in society; the two passages were a long way apart in the book, but the repetition would have been very noticeable if I had left them both in.

Cut chit-chat in your dialogue, remembering that while it must appear natural, a faithful rendition of what your characters would really have said would be full of repetitions, hesitations and deviations – and boring to boot.

Are there any places where your research is showing, by which I mean that you have inserted fascinating background details which really have nothing to do with your story? Then cut them.

Cut your 'habit words'. My first drafts are always

over-larded with 'obviously', 'clearly', and 'of course', and I have to be careful to chop out as many of them as I can.

Pay particular attention to your opening page. Does it hook the reader? Does it get on with the action? Is everything about it relevant? Could the first paragraph disappear without any ill effect? And when you get to the end of the book, could the last paragraph go (which is even more likely)?

Other Revisions

Make sure that you have been consistent – that your heroine's eyes do not change colour, for instance (you might be surprised how often that kind of mistake occurs in beginners' work). All the people in your novel should always behave in character (remember the 'would he really?' test). Look at the timing of the various events in the novel, and make sure that if a scene takes place, for example, in the autumn you have not shown your heroine admiring the daffodils and snowdrops. And have you have been consistent in the spelling of names and in the use of capital letters? I usually make a list, against which I can check that I have always written, let us say, 'Buonaparte' rather than 'Bonaparte', or 'the Meeting House' rather than 'the meeting house'.

Are there any anachronisms in the book? Ensure that you have not used wording which has too modern a feel about it. At the same time, check that you have not been tempted into the use of God-wottery.

Have you under-written, and perhaps missed opportunities by failing to 'make a scene of it'? In one of my novels, one of the major characters died, much to the sorrow of my hero. When my editor saw the book, she pointed out that I should have inserted a moving deathbed scene. Of course, I did so. Incidentally, I always try to take the advice of my editor. I may argue occasionally, but an editor's comments are worth listening to very carefully, and they are usually right. I have had great cause to be grateful to my editors – even to the one who made me take out a whole subplot, involving a cut of close on 20,000 words. The book was much the better for it.

Have you put in appropriate 'little clouds'? Have you cut any 'little clouds' which don't lead anywhere?

Pay particular attention to the first chapter. Does anything in it need changing because of later developments in the story? Perhaps you need to put in a 'little cloud' to prepare for something which happens later.

Look for clumsy phrasing, ill-chosen words, ambiguities. Not only should your prose be economical, but rhythmical and clear, and while you want colour in your writing, you must also aim at a basic simplicity. Your sentences should have a balance in them, by which I mean that there should be a kind of flow in their sequence. At the same time, beware of repetitive rhythms, such as a series of short sentences each of which is constructed in the same way. (Look for these faults when you read the work aloud.)

Are there any overlong paragraphs in the book which would be better split into shorter passages, or broken by dialogue? A long and solid-looking chunk of text is off-putting to many readers.

Check your spelling, punctuation and grammar, and make sure that you have used your words carefully. If you have great difficulty with these tools of the trade, it is worth spending some time in an effort to master them, but if all else fails, get a friend who does understand such matters to correct your mistakes.

Tidying Up

When you have worked your way through that formidable list of possible revisions, there is a final task. Your cuts may sometimes leave obvious gaps, or you may have a later reference in your novel to something which has now disappeared because it was irrelevant. Such things have to be tidied up. You may need to write bridging passages to cover the gaps, or to take out those references which no longer tie up.

Part of the process too is giving the book a final polish, altering a word here, a phrase there. However, as I have already suggested, you should not go on polishing for ever. Once you get into the mood, it is very tempting to go on, but sooner or later you must make the decision that you have done enough.

Your book, when retyped or printed out on your word processor, is then ready for submission to a publisher.

10

GETTING INTO PRINT

You've finished your book, you've revised it until it's just about as good as you can get it, and now you're ready to try to get it published. How do you set about that task?

The Typescript

First of all, do make sure that your book is properly typed or printed in double spacing on one side only, with good margins (at least an inch) all round. Try to make sure that you use the same margin throughout, and that you have the same number of lines on each page.

(Apologies if you've heard the contents of that last paragraph a hundred times before, and it's very boring. You'd be surprised how many ill-typed, almost illegible typescripts publishers still receive despite all modern electronic aides. They don't look professional, and if they're difficult to read you are putting an immediate barrier in the way of the editor's interest.)

The typescript does not have to be perfect – a few corrections are acceptable – but if any of the pages begin to look messy, re-do them.

Number the pages from 1 on to the end. Don't start

again at 1 when you begin a new chapter. You do not need to put the title of the book or the chapter at the head of each page, though it will do no harm if you want to do so.

The title page should show the title, the author's name or pseudonym, and the author's name and address. Include a list of contents if your chapters have titles, a dedication if you want one, and a list of any acknowledgements you need to make, either because you have quoted a published book, or because you wish to thank someone for their help.

It is also a good idea to give an indication of the length of the book in number of words on the title page.

A magazine will normally buy First Serial Rights only, giving them the right to bring out your book for the first time in their magazine, leaving you free to sell it subsequently to a book publisher, whilst a publisher will expect to buy Volume Rights, but you do not need to indicate this on your typescript.

It is worth spending whatever it costs you in time, effort and money to produce a professional-looking typescript.

Market Research

Now you have to decide to which publisher you are going to send your book, or even whether you wish to try and self-publish.

If you are going to self-publish, beware! There are fundamentally two routes – one where you undertake most of the work – either producing a digital book, or arrange for printing and distribution (including selling copies to anyone and at any place and time you can think of). The second route is where a company agrees to do this for you, but will charge a fee for its services. The latter often state they will undertake marketing also – but rarely do so in practice. Don't be fooled! That said, there are occasional success stories that emerge from self-publishing, particularly where the author has been actively networking and spreading the word. However, with hundreds of thousands of titles published each year to add to the millions already in the market place, such successes are very much the occasional exception rather than the rule.

If you wish to go down the conventional publishing route, (and initially you are probably right to do so), do some market research first. Go to your library and to your local bookseller, and find out which publishing houses bring out the kind of book you have written. In some cases, particularly among the larger firms, you may find that they publish a very wide range of historical novels, from the short lightweight romance to the carefully researched, long and complex novel. In other cases, the scope is much more limited, and the publisher may be interested only in romantic stories, or only in something which might be described as scholarly and of very high literary quality.

Don't be afraid to ask advice. Librarians and booksellers (provided that you approach them at a slack time) will probably be very willing to help you.

When you have done your market research, make a list of all the possible publishers. The list can be as long as you like. Some authors are lucky enough to get an offer of publication the very first time that they send their work out; others have to make many attempts before the book is read by a sympathetic editor.

Submission

It is usually advisable to contact a publisher before actually sending the typescript, asking whether you may submit it for consideration. Make it a brief, business-like letter, and enclose a stamped addressed envelope for the reply. Give some indication of what sort of book it is – 'a historical novel about the fictional love-affair between Henry VIII and my imaginary central character, Lady Mary Whatshername' – and say approximately how many thousand words it contains.

You may have to send a number of such letters before you get a favourable reply – it is not easy to break in – but keep on trying.

Once you have found a publisher who is willing to read the book, post it or deliver it to his or her offices, including postage for its return. If you deliver it by hand, don't expect to see the editor. He or she will not want to discuss the novel before reading it, and if you feel that there is something about it that you must explain, then your book is probably already a failure, because it should be capable of standing on its own feet without any additional comments from you.

Now is the time for patience. Publishers in general take an apparently unconscionable time to consider a typescript (though there are often many good reasons for the delay), and you are unlikely to hear anything for at least four to six weeks. Because of this, many authors wonder whether it is possible to send the book to more than one publisher at the same time – to make what is known as a multiple submission.

Nowadays multiple submissions are far more acceptable than they used to be, but it is advisable, when sending in your preliminary letter, to ask whether the publisher would object if you send the book elsewhere at the same time.

If your book comes back to you, don't expect to be given reasons for the rejection. A few publishers will tell you why they are turning it down, but the majority will not. If you are given a critical comment or two, it may well be worth trying to put right whatever is wrong before you send the book out again. On the other hand, if the rejection letter includes any encouraging remarks, you can take them at face value – most publishers do not make a habit of encouraging authors unless they are genuinely interested in their work, although many will issue a 'standard' letter. You need to read 'between the lines' to discern which.

Don't be put off by a rejection. Remember all the stories of bestselling authors who had the devil's own job to get their first acceptance. So persevere. Send the book to the next publisher on your list, and remain optimistic. However, if you receive a whole string of rejections without a single word of encouragement, perhaps you should look at your book again. Since it is probably some time since you read it, you may be able to see for yourself what is wrong, and perhaps you can improve it before you try again.

So far we have been talking of a completed book. It is possible to sell a novel on the basis of two or three specimen chapters, plus a synopsis. It may save the trouble of writing the whole thing without any certainty of publication, which might be a waste of time and effort.

Many publishers are in fact willing to look at a synopsis and specimen chapters, but very few will actually commission a book on such a basis, unless the author has already established some reputation as a novelist. As for encouraging you to continue, you may not get much guidance. If the publisher returns the material saying that he or she is not interested, it does not necessarily mean that the book is no good – it may simply not fit the publisher's requirements at the time. If the response you get is encouraging, it may lift your spirits, but unless the publisher replies in very enthusiastic terms you should not build your expectations too high, and there is no guarantee of eventual publication.

I think most publishers much prefer to see a completed book. Specimen chapters and a synopsis are rarely sufficient for a proper judgement – even if the publisher likes the first couple of chapters, he or she is likely to be wary, having read so many submitted novels which start off well and then fail to fulfil their opening promise.

However, there is nothing to stop you trying this approach if you want to, though I think you may not find it a very rewarding exercise. In any case, I would not agree that to write the book and then fail to find a publisher for it is a waste of time and effort. The more you write, the more you will learn. Besides, you can never call yourself a novelist until you have completed a full-length book, can you?

Agents

Many would-be authors believe that it is impossible to get into print without an agent. This is not true. Publishers do tend to take particular notice of books which come to them from an agent, because they know that if the book is being handled by an agent, it almost certainly has some merit, and that the agent would not have submitted the book if it were not suitable for their list. Nevertheless, thousands of books are accepted by publishers without the involvement of agents.

In any case, the problem is that, generally speaking, it is more difficult for the first-time author to find an agent than to find a publisher. It can be done, however. If you look at a list of agents see the dates when their business was founded, and it is probably advisable to choose one of the newer firms, who are more likely to be looking for clients. Nearly all agents expect a preliminary letter of enquiry first, and some of them charge a reading fee.

One of the main reasons why beginners want an agent

is because it saves them from doing any market research – it is part of an agent's job to know which publishers are likely to be interested in a given book. However, if you undertake your own submissions to publishers and eventually receive an offer of publication, you may then find it much easier to get an agent to take you on, and you will certainly find that there are great advantages in being represented in this way. It is not that the publisher will cheat the un-agented author – most publishers value their reputation too highly to behave badly, and the few rotten apples in the barrel are usually just as appalling whether an agent is involved or not – but an agent can often negotiate better terms, and will of course check the contract on your behalf to make sure that everything in it is fair. He or she will also be ready to do many other things for you, including, for instance, undertaking the possible sale of translation and other subsidiary rights in your work, and sometimes securing for you commissions to write other books. A good agent will also often offer you editorial advice.

Although, as already mentioned, some agents charge a reading fee, the majority do not expect any payment from you until your writings which they have handled begin to earn money. Then they will take their cut, which is usually ten to fifteen per cent, but in some cases is at a higher rate, especially on foreign sales.

A question which frequently arises is whether an agent, when taking on a new client, will ask him or her to sign a formal agreement. A few may do so, but it is more likely that correspondence will be exchanged, in which the agent sets out his terms, and the author agrees to them. The terms will include, for instance, the percentages that the agent will take on earnings, and the understanding that, while the author will be free to leave the agency at any time, the agent will continue to take those percentages on any contracts which he or she negotiated and which still remain in force.

The Publisher's Contract

When a publisher decides to take your book, he or she will probably write to you first setting out the proposed terms. The letter may not go much beyond telling you what sum is offered as an advance against the eventual earnings of the book, and what royalty rates will be paid on sales of the publisher's own edition. Only when the contract arrives will you see all the details, including the split of moneys earned by subsidiary rights (such as paperback editions, book clubs, film sale etc.), provisions, if any, for consultation with you about the jacket of the book, and a host of other matters. A publisher's contract is nowadays a highly complicated legal document, and although in most cases you can be reasonably certain that it will not be grossly unfair to you, it is worth taking advice before you sign it. If you have an agent, he or she will vet the contract, and you should have no difficulties. If you do not have an agent, you can get free expert advice by joining a Society of Authors or Writers. You could also, of course, go to a lawyer, but in that case it is worth going to one who specialises in the publishing business and fully understands the niceties of a publisher's contract. Another possibility is to ask a friend who is experienced in these matters (perhaps a published author whom you know through your local Writers' Circle) to check the document for you.

Remember that an agreement from a publisher is open to negotiation. If you think that the publisher ought to be offering better terms, or if there is anything in the contract which you do not like or even understand, don't be afraid to ask him or her about it. You may be told that the point you query is 'standard publishing practice' or the answer may simply blind you with science, but as long as you put your questions courteously, you will not harm your relationship with the publisher. Despite your fears, publishers do not change their minds and refuse to publish just because you ask a few polite questions and indicate that there are certain things in the contract which puzzle you or which sound less than fair.

Copyright

The copyright in your book is yours as soon as you write it. You should never surrender your copyright. If a publisher offers to buy your book 'outright', you should not agree. Ask for a royalty agreement, however tempting the sum he proposes may sound. It will be better for you in the end.

A Final Word

In order to get published as a historical novelist you need first and foremost a certain amount of talent as a writer. You need to be able to tell an interesting story, with believable characters in whose problems and adventures your reader can become involved, and a background which has a true period atmosphere. You should also ask yourself whether you are truly a novelist – have you got the stamina to produce a well-constructed story of book length, or are you really much happier with the short story, despite the difficulties of that genre? And you should have striven to achieve a degree of originality in the story itself, the characters and the setting, and have tried to make it your own book rather than an imitation of some popular writer's work. It is also essential for you to be very self-critical, so that you try your hardest to see the weaknesses in your novel and then keep working at it until you have eliminated the faults as far as you possibly can. At the same time you must have enough confidence in yourself and your ability to go on trying to find a publisher for the book despite initial failures to do so.

Even if your book meets every criterion to make it publishable, there is one other thing you need – a little bit of luck. You need the luck of sending the typescript to a publisher whose editor is not only in sympathy with the type of novel you have written, and likes the way you have done it, but who is looking for just that sort of thing at the very time that your book turns up on his or her desk.

The last thing that I have to say, therefore, is – good luck!

Michael Legat

Mario's Vineyard

Frustrated with his father's strict control and hankering after freedom, Mario Gilardone could see no way of ever leaving his home in northern Italy. But that was before the 'phylloxera' disease struck, devastating the family's prosperous vineyards. Seizing the opportunity, he decided to leave his country, and the girl he loved, and set sail for America to set up his own vineyard in the sunny, fertile soils of California.

Like so many others in the great nineteenth-century exodus from Europe, Mario arrived to a hostile New York hungry and penniless. He was soon to learn the harsh realities of a foreign land, but his pride and fierce ambition kept the dream of Mario's Vineyard alive. He would succeed no matter what.

The Silk Maker

In a time when working conditions were renowned for their harsh cruelty, Harcourts' silk mill surpassed them all with its relentless and unforgiving regime – a regime so brutal that it sent men to an early grave and left families destitute.

After such conditions had caused his own father's death, Richard Goodwin seemed destined for the workhouse. In a final bid for freedom, he journeyed to a neighbouring town to find work in a rival mill. There he acquired the secrets and skills of the silk trade, and found that his new knowledge had also brought him power. For when their fortunes were reversed and it was the Harcourts facing severe hardship, Richard had a choice – to take revenge once and for all or to offer help and reconciliation. But could he make the right decision when Sarah Harcourt featured so heavily in his mind?

Michael Legat

The Cast Iron Man

From an early age Edward Harcourt knew that he was expected to devote his life to his late father's silk-making business. Failing this, the only other option open to him was to join his 'Uncle' Richard in Norfolk and specialise in brocade. Neither choice appealed – but what did interest him was the mystery surrounding this 'Uncle' Richard. When the long-hidden truth finally emerged, Edward fled in horror from the certain knowledge of his parentage, and found himself in London ready to start a new life. Desperate to distance himself from his family's industry, he opted for work in the manufacture of cast-iron fireplaces and curios. There he found considerable success – and an escape from his mother's suffocating grasp.

Set in the last years of the nineteenth century *The Cast Iron Man* continues the turbulent saga of the Harcourt and Goodwin families first introduced in *The Silk Maker*.

The Silver Fountain

Ambitious and talented Jean-Paul Fontaine had one overwhelming desire – to run an exclusive restaurant in London. His path was beset with frustration and tragedy but in time he rose from the penniless young waiter he had been when he arrived in London to the proprietor of The Silver Fountain – a delightful restaurant in a quiet street in Soho.

The Silver Fountain was to prove only the beginning of a long-standing and intense relationship between the Fontaine family and the restaurant world. Moving through the generations from the 1870s to the 1930s, and from London to Paris and New York, this is a passionate tale of obsession, ambition and culinary creation.

Printed in Great Britain
by Amazon

82138998R00072